PRAISE FOR SEASONS

Grief, healing, hope, loss and love. Celina's words will resonate with the wild nature of each changing season in your life and mine. Each chapter in *Seasons* will stir up your weary faith, cause you to lean into truth once again, and encourage you deep in your bones to be fully present in the season you find yourself in because, 'For everything there is a season, and a time for every matter under heaven'.

Andi Andrew, United States of America
Author, Speaker and Podcaster

I love this book! It is so helpful. Celina writes brilliantly and vulnerably on a subject that affects all of our lives. I often hear people say 'it's just a season' when they are attempting to help us feel better about the seemingly unending change or challenge we are going through. Celina brings solid insight and clarity to this concept of life seasons, drawing from her wealth of biblical knowledge and practical personal stories of trouble, triumph and transition. As I have gotten to know Celina in recent years, I have observed her calm, godly tenacity in life as a mum and minister, business owner and encouraging destiny friend. I can highly recommend her as being uniquely qualified to help you identify the gold that can be found in every season that contributes to this wonderful God-given adventure of life.

Rachel Mawston, United Kingdom
Author, Speaker and Leadership Coach

Celina and I first met in 2021 when I attended a service she was preaching in. I remember vividly how her sermon convicted me of the importance of obedience to Christ. With her new book, Celina continues to give me precious insights into how to live my faith as a Christian. As seasons of life come and go, we must embrace every change and be swift to adapt so we can seize every single day in every season. Definitely the right book to read!

Greysia Polii, Indonesia
Athlete and Olympic Gold Medallist

As I read this book, my first thought was *Celina truly gets it*! She has an amazing gift to put into words what we all have felt and experienced – namely, trying to navigate life's twists and turns! Through personal stories, insightful reflections and biblical truths, *Seasons: Stories of Loss, Light, Hope and Harvest* provides both comfort and guidance as you and I navigate through life's different seasons. Most importantly, Celina shows how no season is wasted. In each season, God invites us to experience His faithfulness and to learn even more what it means to follow Jesus through the highs and lows of life. As the pastor of the church where Celina is a member and a highly valued preacher, I already know Celina to be an inspired communicator who speaks with wisdom and honesty. Therefore, I am extra thrilled that she now has written her first book so that more people will get to know the message that God has put on her heart; it's a message that will help you on your faith journey.

Eric Andersson, Denmark
Lead Pastor of ARK CPH

Celina Mina is a rare gem, traversing life's landscape with an unyielding quest for meaning and purpose. In her book, *Seasons: Stories of Loss, Light, Hope and Harvest*, she emerges as a master wordsmith, a purveyor of wonder and a connoisseur of beauty. Through the seamless fusion of personal narratives and profound reflections on faith, she crafts a rich and heartfelt exploration of life's ebbs and flows. Her words offer solace and inspiration, gracefully guiding readers through the realms of grief, calling, love and motherhood with unparalleled authenticity. As a beacon of hope, this book illuminates the path towards redemption and fulfilment in every season of life. May it captivate you as it did me, becoming a cherished companion, with dog-eared pages and full of markings and underlinings. I am confident that it will become 'that book' so easily shared with friends navigating their own highs and lows on the journey of life.

Cass Langton, Australia
Co-Founder of The Hopeful Rhino

Celina is a wordsmith. She does to words what Gordon Ramsay or Jamie Oliver does to a host of ingredients – she turns them into a delicious meal that you want to experience over and over again. Not everyone can do that! This book distils years of wisdom and life experience into something you can easily read and relate to. It allows you to interpret and sometimes reinterpret your life experience in a positive way. Using the natural seasons of winter, spring, summer and autumn as a metaphor for the changing seasons of life, we are taken on a journey of how to recognise and even embrace the benefit each season offers. The winter seasons of life (and there is more than one) don't seem fruitful, but they do prepare the way for another season. Above all, this book will give you hope. Hope that, as you embrace the season of life you are currently in and learn its powerful lessons, you are preparing yourself for a new season. And a new season will come, bringing growth, maturity and understanding. The only question left to answer is, 'Can you embrace it and learn the lessons God wants to teach you through it?' I heartily recommend it to you as a great read and a helpful tool in your journey of life.

Peter Prothero, United Kingdom
Equippers Global Team; Author, Speaker and Leadership Coach

SEASONS

STORIES OF LOSS, LIGHT, HOPE AND HARVEST

Celina Evelyn Mina

Seasons: Stories of Loss, Light, Hope and Harvest

All reasonable efforts have been made to provide accurate sources and reference details for other literary works quoted in this publication. Any discrepancies or omissions will be rectified in future editions.

This book is a memoir. It reflects the author's present recollections of experiences over time. Some names and characteristics have been omitted, some events have been compressed, and some dialogue has been recreated.

First printing 2024
Cataloguing – in – Publication data available

ISBN 978-87-975162-0-1 (paperback)
ISBN 978-87-975162-1-8 (e-book)

Cover design: Hazel Lam
Interior design: Carlos Darby [www.AbruptStudio.com]
Photography: Sylva Bocsa
Proof-Editor: Yasmin Yarwood [www.meticulousproofreading.co.uk]

For Kathy – see you on the other side,
where there is no more weeping.

To Annika and Frederik – the future is bright
and you are both deeply loved.

CONTENTS

PART V – TRANSITION'S VALUE

Can you dare to believe that God's story about you
puts your story in spiritual perspective?
One way to do this is to write down your personal story
without editing out your vulnerability and brokenness
and to be willing to tell your story to others.
This is the discipline of witness in the world.

Henri Nouwen[1]

I have on my table a violin string. It is free to move
in any direction I like.
If I twist one end it responds; it is free.
But it is not free to sing.
So, I take it and fix it into my violin.
I bind it and when it is bound, it is free for the first time to sing.

Rabindranath Tagore[2]

PREFACE:

Vivaldi Understood...

October 2022, Paris, Autumn

The fact you chose to pick up this book and have started to read it blows me away. This book contains the words I'd love to say to you if we were sitting opposite each other in a café having an unrushed conversation. Speaking of cafés – the waiter and barista at Maison Fleuret recognise me now. A cappuccino, a glass of water, a slice of their homemade lemon and poppyseed loaf, my notebook and pencil, and my laptop. I've turned up three mornings in a row to plan and begin writing the book you are now holding in your hands.

Among the sounds of the coffee machine and French chatter, classical music plays as the soundtrack for this delightful café. I close my eyes, and it takes me back in time. I started playing the violin when I was seven years old. Back in 1988. By the time I reached my teenage years, I was playing in the Melbourne Youth Orchestras in Australia, and by the time I reached my early twenties, I'd qualified as a secondary school music and English teacher. While I currently don't play my violin as much as I used to do, and while I no longer teach music full-time in a classroom, the work of one baroque composer, Antonio Vivaldi, has forever left its mark on my soul.

At the age of sixteen, I learned to perform *Winter* from Vivaldi's *The Four Seasons*. It's one of four concerti for violin. I'm guessing you know the names of the other three, right? You got it – *Spring*, *Summer* and *Autumn*. With each concerto comprising three movements, this composition really captivated my interest in understanding the seasons. Vivaldi desired to express the uniqueness of each season through music – the sounds and the silences – and he based his composition on four sonnets about the seasons, which he also wrote. Excerpts of the poems appear throughout the sheet music, guiding the violinist's understanding and interpretation.

In November 2018, I wrote and preached a Sunday sermon at the church I was attending at that time. The title of the sermon was *Welcome, Winter*. An odd time of the year for an Australian to be focusing on winter, you may be thinking. Well, I was no longer in Melbourne. I had just started my seventh year of living in Copenhagen, Denmark. And winter had arrived, indeed! By then, I had experienced six complete cycles of the seasons in the Northern Hemisphere. And what Vivaldi taught me as a teenager through his music is true: every season is enchanting and . . . necessary.

Back to preaching at church. As you've perhaps figured out, I'm a words and music person. I'm also a Christian – a follower of Jesus. And the words of the Bible teach us a lot about the seasons. God created them after all. The thing is, the essential question I grappled with throughout the first four decades of my life – and perhaps it's a question you struggle with also – is this: if God is really at work in our lives, how can we see His active involvement in our circumstances? I believe that when we apply to our inner world what nature's seasons teach us, we begin to see that every situation, event, heartache, relationship and success leads to meaning, redemption and fulfilment. But this takes time, patience and, most of all, the grace of God.

The church congregation gave me a lot of positive feedback on that sermon. It struck a chord. I felt it. They felt it. I knew I couldn't stop there. In March 2019, I preached a sermon called *It's Time for Spring*. I think you can see where this is going. July soon arrived, bringing with it the sermon *Summer Is Calling*. Finally, *Autumn Has Arrived* concluded the year-long series in the October of 2019. 'You should write a book about this, Celina!' people enthusiastically said to me. *Really?* I smiled politely and thanked them for the encouragement. A couple more years went by. I clearly needed a few more orbits around the sun for God to really get it into my head that writing this book was something I needed to do – to glorify Him, to grow spiritually and to encourage others.

The main message that weaved through all four sermons is this: He is faithful in every season of your life and uses every season of your life for good – even when you can't see it or feel it. This can be hard to believe. As I write this, I am mindful that many people around the world live under sustained oppression. Many people face long-term suffering. Tragedy beyond belief. If this book has found its way into such a set of circumstances, my prayer is that the revelation of Christ crucified and resurrected will fill your heart and bring tangible peace. He is with you.

No matter where you're at in your discipleship journey, I want the words of this book to give you encouragement, support, wisdom and strength. You may have picked up this book because you have a growing awareness that God has more for your life, and a desire to step into everything He has created, saved and called you for. Or, you may have picked up this book because you're discouraged and disappointed by how your life is currently looking – nothing like you imagined. You feel stuck. Perhaps you're trying to make sense of everything that's unfolding (and truth be told, unravelling) around you and inside you; you're confused, weary and deflated, but feel ashamed or embarrassed to admit it. After all, we Christians should have it all together, right? But what if what you're feeling and going through doesn't mean there's something 'wrong' with you? Or that something's 'wrong' with your faith? What if it's actually the very catalyst that God is going to use to transform your life? What if the four seasons are softly, yet urgently, calling out to you?

Autumn's loss. Winter's light. Spring's hope. Summer's harvest.

Vivaldi ordered them differently (spring, summer, autumn, winter). However, if harvest is the goal, loss must be the start. You'll understand why as you read on.

These pages will offer you a perspective and a biblical framework to inform your mindset and approach regarding your life. At the time of writing, I've been on the planet for just over four decades. This 'halfway' milestone caused me to reflect on four major life stories I have lived so far, each with their own seasons and a quest for revelation:
A story of grief and healing – *where is God in my grief and suffering?*
A story of calling – *what is God doing with my life?*
A story of love – *does God want me to experience love?*
A story of motherhood – *will God help me raise the next generation?*

I don't have all the answers (I'm a work in progress, just like you!), but I'm bravely choosing to share snippets from different seasons of these stories with you in the hope that my vulnerability and the work of God in my life will stir up your faith, teach you His truth, encourage you with wisdom, and inspire you to get out there and make the most of the grand adventure God has set before you.

Simply, this is the story of an ordinary everyday woman who has taken faith steps that haven't always turned out the way she envisaged. I'm sure you'll relate because seasons unite us – they come and go. I hope you can link your story to mine. And discover that, ultimately, within His story we discover our own. So, dear reader, your seasons and stories await you.

INTRODUCTION

Every Season Has a Story to Tell

What is your favourite season? Autumn? Winter? Spring? Summer? *Why* is it your favourite season? Perhaps you look forward to getting out the woollen jumpers in autumn, lighting candles in winter, seeing flowers blossom in spring or diving into a pool in summer. Well, here's something about me that's maybe a little bit strange . . .

I no longer have a favourite season.

Yes, you read that correctly. My favourite season used to be summer, for obvious reasons – holidays, travel, the beach, sunshine, ice cream, afternoon naps. While I still enjoy and look forward to summer and holidays, I've come to profoundly realise that if I want to get the most out of life all year round, then I need to make *every* season my favourite season. That sounds obvious, but difficult in practice. However, our inner world goes through seasons just like our world goes through the rhythm of four seasons each year. And just as we experience the natural seasons of our geographical climate and environment, so too does our inner world go through continually changing seasons. As King Solomon in Scripture explains,

> For everything there is a season, and a time for every matter under heaven:
> a time to be born, and a time to die;
> a time to plant, and a time to pluck up what is planted;
> a time to kill, and a time to heal;
> a time to break down, and a time to build up;

a time to weep, and a time to laugh;
a time to mourn, and a time to dance;
a time to cast away stones, and a time to gather stones together;
a time to embrace, and a time to refrain from embracing;
a time to seek, and a time to lose;
a time to keep, and a time to cast away;
a time to tear, and a time to sew;
a time to keep silence, and a time to speak;
a time to love, and a time to hate;
a time for war, and a time for peace.

Ecclesiastes 3:1–8 ESV

A time for everything. But not everything at the same time.

Society convinces and urges us that we can have it all – and have it now. The instant access into other people's lives through scrolling on social media, combined with targeted advertising strategies and algorithms, all upon the foundation of our formative childhood experiences, can easily entice us into the traps the enemy has laid out for humanity since the Garden of Eden[3] – doubt and discontentment. When comparison creeps in and triggers feelings of not being good enough and not deserving good things, we begin to look at our own circumstances through the lens of doubt (*why isn't my faith working?*) and discontentment (*what is everyone else getting right that I'm getting wrong?*). We can forget that seasons are part of God's creation. Psalm 74:14 states: 'It was you who set all the boundaries of the earth; you made both summer and winter.' Seasons are also part of God's covenant: 'As long as the earth endures, seedtime and harvest, cold and heat, summer and winter, day and night will never cease' (Genesis 8:22). Therefore, life is lived in seasons. And while some places around the world joke about the weather being like 'four seasons in one day', we appreciate that one location in one point of time cannot be in autumn, winter, spring and summer at once. We need that same understanding of and approach to our personal lives, dear reader. Why? To have our eyes and ears opened to the stories every season is trying to tell us. Stories that ultimately reveal the faithfulness and active involvement of God in our lives.

Recognise your season

I wrote earlier that our inner world goes through seasons just like our world goes through the rhythm of four seasons each year. The thing is, we could experience spring on the outside, but go through autumn on the inside. Or winter on the outside, but summer on the inside. (That sounds nice.) Proverbs, the Book of Wisdom, instructs us to 'know the importance of the season you're in' (10:5 TPT). We need to understand *why* each season is important, then intentionally change our attitude towards some of our current 'least favourite' seasons. We need to become good at recognising the seasons we're going through in order to approach the different areas of our lives with wisdom and intentionality. If we don't pay attention to the shifting seasons in our inner world, we can become frustrated and misunderstand what God may be wanting to do in and through us.

It's hard, though, isn't it? To embrace every season. We would love summer all year round. People move to parts of the world or live six months in one place and six in another to have sunshine and warmth for as long as possible. Perhaps you know people who do that. Maybe you are one of those people (no judgement!). I can imagine it's more pleasant and comfortable than facing autumn and winter. I get it. Far more exciting than witnessing the faint glimmers of spring. However, this is what I know now:

The pain and preparation of *loss*,
the process of learning in the dark how to be *light*,
and holding onto the promises of *hope*
are *all* needed to finally gather in the *harvest*.

Autumn leads to winter,
which leads to spring,
which leads to summer.

Time leads to invitation,
which leads to decision,
which leads to action.

And there are always lessons to learn.

Fighting against this rhythm will cause you to fight against your own soul. The natural world needs the seasons. And so do you.

How to read this book

This book is intended to become a companion that hangs around for a while as you live through some seasons of your own. Part I focuses on Autumn's Loss, Part II on Winter's Light, Part III on Spring's Hope and Part IV on Summer's Harvest. There is also Part V, which is dedicated to an 'underrated season' – Transition's Value. Each part consists of four chapters – twenty chapters altogether – opening with personal storytelling. The teaching sections that follow the stories highlight the role of time, invitation, decision, action and lessons within our spiritual formation as Christ's followers. 'Reflect on Your Season – Journaling Prompts and Practical Tips' is provided at the end of the book, allowing you to reflect on your story, too.

My prayer for you is that you will decide to look forward to every part of the year and make every season your favourite season so that you don't remain wounded from your past, avoid your present nor fear your future, but curiously surrender each season to the Lord, trusting Him to make all things beautiful at the proper time.[4]

PART I —

Autumn's Loss

Allegro
Celebrates the peasant, with songs and dances,
The pleasure of a bountiful harvest.
And fired up by Bacchus' liquor,
Many end their revelry in sleep.

Adagio molto
Everyone is made to forget their cares and to sing and dance
By the air which is tempered with pleasure
And (by) the season that invites so many, many
Out of their sweetest slumber to fine enjoyment.

Allegro
The hunters emerge at the new dawn,
And with horns and dogs and guns depart upon their hunting.
The beast flees and they follow its trail;
Terrified and tired of the great noise
Of guns and dogs. The beast, wounded, threatens
Languidly to flee, but harried, dies.[5]

PRELUDE –

Time

In Denmark, the weeks on calendars are numbered, from week one to week fifty-two. It can take a little getting used to, but it becomes very helpful when you finally get your head around it. Week forty-two is autumn break in Copenhagen. Every year. The sunshine of summer is a distant memory; jackets and scarves on display in shop windows are a reminder of what's ahead. Autumn is a funny season – it's both a bridge between the two extremes and a season in its own right. As a result, it's a time that brings up a range of feelings: nervousness, disappointment, restlessness, worry, anticipation, relief, to name a few.

Yet while our earthly lives are linear, we need to remember that God is eternal. Consider these words from Psalm 139:5 (TPT):

> You've gone into my future to prepare the way,
> and in kindness you follow behind me
> to spare me from the harm of my past.
> With your hand of love upon my life,
> you impart a blessing to me.

How is that possible? Our current earthly lives exist within time. Yesterday was the past; today is the present; tomorrow is the future. It's linear. God, however, is eternal. He created time. He is not limited by time. He is outside of time and Jesus entered into time as part of taking on the limitations of humanity. Ultimately, God is 'the Alpha and the

Omega, the First and the Last, the Beginning and the End' (Revelation 22:13 NLT). We simply cannot get our heads around this. Our linear thinking is limited; our linear thinking cannot understand the eternal ways of an eternal God. However, during autumn, we can trust His supernatural ability to divinely orchestrate our lives where things from our past which, from a linear perspective, are over, can, from an eternal perspective, play a vital role within our future.

Here are four observations about the natural season of autumn which I believe will help you recognise and understand autumn when it arrives in your inner world:

1. A time of shifts and change
2. A time of mystery and unknowns
3. A time of preservation and protection
4. A time of letting go and comfort

Remember, this sacred season is about understanding the pain and preparation of loss.

All will be well. Just give it time.

CHAPTER 1:

Grief and Healing – The Day It All Fell Apart

October 2019, Copenhagen, Autumn

The psychiatrist sat back in her chair and looked at me, empathy in her eyes. After a few moments of silence, which felt like eternity, she gave me what I came for. A diagnosis. I wanted it, and I didn't want it. I wanted it so I could be put out of my misery, and I didn't want it because I knew it would make me more miserable. These situations always seem to be lose-lose when you've hit rock bottom. I'd just never expected to hit rock bottom at thirty-eight years old. But as they say, the only way up is down.

'Stress-induced moderate depression,' she said calmly. 'You will need to be on full-time sick leave for at least three months. Probably four. But we will wait and see. No teaching, no volunteering at your church, no work of any kind. And I want to see you once a week for a while.' *Depression? Sick leave? Three months? Maybe four? No work of any kind? Weekly therapy?!* Disbelief, panic and overwhelm set in. This was worse than I'd thought. I'd been hoping that a two-week holiday in a tropical location would do the trick. Clearly not. Tears streaming down my face, I wrote down the details for my next session. I didn't need to check if I was available – after all, as of that moment, I had nothing on for the next four months.

Just like that, autumn had walked into my life to stay for a while, in the form of a mental health diagnosis, completely uninvited, bringing with it unwelcome change.

* * *

Kathy, my half-sister, who I always saw as my full sister, passed away from cancer in the August of 2016 while I was on maternity leave with my second child. The final eight years of her life were filled with tragic health complications and indescribable heartache, which took an almost unbearable toll on our family, especially on our courageous dad, Clifford Fitt. Her funeral took place in the early part of the September, and I went back to work – with my son beginning *vuggestue* (Danish nursery) – shortly afterwards. I was thirty-five years old.

It didn't take long before I was swept away by the tidal wave of raising two young children (a five-year-old daughter and a one-year-old son) and fulfilling commitments in other areas of my life while my husband, Andrew, was back at work. If that wasn't enough, other things were thrown into the mix during the following twelve months: some of our closest friends moved away, Andrew was made redundant, the rental agreement on our apartment ended, and I experienced a stressful series of professional challenges in my workplace. Then, a devastating discovery – a rock that splashed into my heart, with an everlasting ripple effect. Compounding all of this was the impact of a wide range of undealt-with issues from my past, which I was oblivious to at the time. Needless to say, I wasn't much fun to be around.

In light of all this, maybe you can understand that I never really had time to properly grieve the death of my sister. Perhaps you know what it's like to go through seemingly never-ending seasons, where you feel like it's just one thing after another. I've read it described as the 'wall' or the 'dark night of the soul' or the 'wilderness' or the 'valley'. Whatever you call it, it's relentless and exhausting. And we all cope in different ways. For me, I shut down my emotions and focused on getting tasks done. Work became my drug to numb the trauma. Tick another thing off the checklist and feel the rush of the dopamine hit. Productivity and Accomplishment were always by my side with the warning, 'Don't sit down for too long or the memories will surface along with the unspeakable pain.' I listened to them. And I paid the price.

* * *

By the time I ended up in my psychiatrist's clinic that sunny, yet chilly, Saturday afternoon in October 2019, I was in a state of breakdown. My hair was falling out, my eyes were continually twitching, and I was waking up each morning with a knot in my chest that literally took my breath away at times. I was unmotivated, filled with fatigue and couldn't remember the last time I'd laughed with joy. Being asked to make a simple decision would quickly reduce me to tears, and, for the life of me, I could never remember where I put my keys. As Bessel van der Kolk aptly titled his book, the body really does 'keep the score'.[6] And the score was not in my favour. Stress-induced depression: one. Celina Evelyn Mina: nil.

* * *

It all sounds very bleak, doesn't it? It was. At the time. But what you also need to know is that even when it felt like everything had fallen apart around me and was shifting on the inside of me, there was still the faintest glimmer of peace and hope. How was that possible? I think one of the reasons was that I started a daily gratitude journal. As counter-intuitive as it was, I found at least one thing I was thankful for and wrote it down. I also reminded myself of what God had already done in my life up to that point – and daring to believe that He would come through for me yet again. You see, when autumn enters our inner world, bringing with it great shifts and change, it can also remind us that God remains the same. Even while suffering from stress-induced moderate depression, I experienced His unchanging nature as my secure foundation.

A time of shifts and change

Leaves change colour. The gradual shift from hues of green to vibrant reds and oranges to golden brown is stunning. A crisp chill in the air makes its annual appearance, and the number of daylight hours decreases.

We also go through shifts and change, don't we? Something ends and something new begins. Sometimes by choice, often not. New studies, a new job, a promotion and new title, a change in finances, a new relationship status, the birth of a child, the death of a loved one, a diagnosis, a relocation to a foreign city, a household in conflict. All resulting in new sets of life circumstances. Regardless of what it may be, it can take a while to settle into a new rhythm and routine. Whether for the better or for the worse, shifts and change can cause overwhelm as our brains work overtime to process these new events and implications. Our brains don't like uncertainty. They will do what they can to create certainty. However, autumn cannot be figured out like a mathematical equation. One plus one does not necessarily equal two in autumn. And that can be difficult, right?

When autumn enters your inner world, bringing with it shifts and change, be reminded of and reflect on this, dear reader:

God remains the same.

Malachi 3:6a says: 'I the Lord do not change...' The writer of Hebrews proclaims that 'Jesus Christ is the same yesterday and today and forever' (13:8). The book of James reassures us that 'every good and perfect gift is from above, coming down from the Father of the heavenly lights, who does not change like shifting shadows' (1:17).

The Lord's faithfulness is unchanging. His holiness and love are unchanging. His plans and purposes for your life are unchanging. His nature and sovereignty remain the same, even when everything else around you is shifting and changing. With this resounding in your soul, you can face what tomorrow holds. You can face grief and walk towards healing.

CHAPTER 2:

Calling – The Hallway, Suitcases and a Violin

May 1988, Melbourne, Autumn

There was not enough room for a piano in my childhood home, so that wasn't an option. Aware of my growing interest in music and desire to play an instrument, my dad came home from the local library with a stack of books containing pictures of instruments. I was captivated – each page presented another possibility. 'Can I learn them all?' The innocence and naivety of children. 'Let's start with one,' my dad chuckled. Furrowed brow with concentration. A big decision in the making for a seven-year-old who didn't like to make mistakes. I never liked letting my parents down. I knew deep down they wanted me to have the type of upbringing they hadn't been able to experience. Loving intention by adults absorbed as pressure by a child. That's when I met the violin and bow. Chestnut brown, delicate yet powerful. Sound qualities resembling the human voice. 'That one!' I pointed at the picture eagerly. I had made my decision and chosen the violin. Or rather, the violin had chosen me.

* * *

'What is she doing?' 'She's got the bags again.' 'She's really into that game!' My mum and dad whispered among themselves, trying to work out why their five-year-old was marching up and down the long, tiled hallway in our house. Arms full of 'luggage' and 'travel documents' in my hand, I kept on marching. I refused to be late for my 'flight'. Finally understanding the game, my dad asked, 'Celina, where are you travelling to today?' 'I'm going to Europe!' I declared without thinking. No idea where it was. The words just flew out of my mouth as I kept marching up and down the 'airport', determined not to miss the flight bound for my future.

* * *

My earliest childhood memories are of the many games of make-believe I'd lose myself in for hours at a time. The airport game was one of them. Another was the library and classroom game. I'd cut up squares of paper, stapling them together to make little books. Too young to read or write, I'd simply draw line after line of squiggles with my coloured pencils. And a pretty picture on the front cover, of course. My teddy bears and dolls would sit obediently in rows, enthralled by their teacher, who had promised them a trip to the library to borrow a new book for the week.

Fast forward to grade three at Holy Trinity Primary School. 1989. My literacy skills were certainly more advanced by then, writing letters of the alphabet instead of colourful squiggles. Students were given book catalogues every month to take home to their parents. Glossy pages showing the covers of the most recently published books for primary-aged children that could be purchased and delivered to the school. The very first chapter book for young readers I ever read was about a gymnast who was really hard on herself. She placed her identity in her ability to perform. If she didn't win first place, she'd failed. It wasn't until a set of tough challenges (every protagonist needs complication to bring about their development before the resolution, right?) that she realised her family and friends love her for who she is, even when she doesn't come first. I read it many times during grade three. Something in me sensed the message was important as a beginner violinist. The title? *Nobody's Perfect.*[7]

Fast forward to grade five. 1991. I was now ten years old. Mrs Piper – one of the best teachers I have ever had. It wouldn't be until I was at Monash University studying to become a teacher that I'd understand just how ahead of her time she was when it came to classroom management and curriculum delivery. Funny and friendly, firm and fair. And an encourager of little dreams. She was safe. She once handed out sheets of paper to the class, saying we had twenty minutes to answer the questions. I panicked. How did I not know we had a test that day? Seeing the worry flash through my eyes, Mrs Piper paused in front of my desk. 'It's okay, Celina. This isn't a graded test.' I looked down at the paper. Question one. *What do you like about yourself?* I blinked, confused. Question two. *What do you think you're good at?* I raised my eyebrows as I squirmed in my wooden chair. Question three. *What is one thing you've never done before that you'd like to try?* It was at that point I realised I was holding my breath.

'Celina, can I talk to you for a minute?' The bell had rung, and my friends were heading out the door for playtime. My default was to immediately think I'd done something wrong. Mrs Piper knew this about me – that I desperately wanted to please the adults in my life. Keep the pride in their eyes. She was holding my paper from the other day. 'You wrote that you'd like to try teaching the class something,' she began with a smile on her face. I looked back blankly. I didn't know where this was going. 'Well, I'm giving you forty-five minutes next week during our writing lesson. We're going to swap places. You can be the teacher, and I'll sit in your seat and be one of the students. You can teach us whatever you want. Just connect it to writing.' My mouth was now hanging wide open. I still hadn't said anything. Mrs Piper laughed gently, almost looking through me, at a future version of myself.

* * *

Light-brown, wavy hair. Kind, brown eyes. I couldn't stop staring at her. Smiling knowingly, she looked down at the possession I was guarding. My little violin case securely nestled next to my feet as I sat with my parents at an airport gate waiting to board our flight from Melbourne to London via a stop in South-East Asia to refuel. My first trip to Europe, at the age of nine! All those games in the hallway had somehow paid off. This woman understood why I was alert, protecting my prized possession. Her adult-sized violin case rested on her lap, forming a little table for the sheet music she was studying. *How long has she been playing the violin? Where does she live? Is she travelling to London to perform at a concert?* I had only been playing for a year. I had little calluses on the ends of my left fingers to prove it.

'I'm Jane,' she said warmly. 'What's your name?' That's all I needed. For the next hour, as we waited to board the plane, I talked and talked and talked and asked her question after question after question, to the amusement of those listening. Jane patiently answered everything I asked her – at one point, she even opened her case in the middle of the airport lounge and got out her violin to explain transitioning from first to third position. I was captivated. When I grew up, I was going to be like Jane. An Australian violinist travelling the world performing and making her way back to Paris, where she lived. I couldn't contain my excitement when, after finally taking off and being free to unbuckle our seatbelts, she came and found me. My childhood self was yet to understand her intentional kindness – and God clearly at work. She had an empty seat next to her and was going to read through the sheet music for her next concert. Would I be interested in sitting next to her and seeing the score? My parents didn't see me again until we got ready to land in South-East Asia.

* * *

'Hang on, you met *who*?' My violin teacher, Elizabeth, was stunned. We were back from our European holiday, and I was back in her music room for my first lesson since arriving home. I was in the middle of telling her all about this woman whom I'd met at the airport and who had given me her address in Paris. She'd promised that if I ever wrote to her, she would write back, and that when she was next in Melbourne, she would get me some tickets for one of her concerts. Elizabeth, clearly seeing that her student didn't understand the enormity of this encounter, placed one hand on my shoulder to get my attention. 'Celina, your *pen pal* is one of Australia's most famous violinists. That's why she now lives in Paris; that's where you go to become the very best!' I grew silent; my eyes widened. It was settled then. When I grew up, I was going back to Europe; I was going to live in Paris and become a famous violinist just like Jane Peters, performing on stages for audiences all around the world.

* * *

Have you ever tried to move a toddler when they're sprawled on the floor and refusing to get up? Nearly impossible. It's easier to guide them when they're already walking. You can gently place your hand on their back, their arm, and set their trajectory. Childhood dreams and desires are the first compass we have. God gets us moving so He can begin to steer us in the right direction. The way He works is a mystery, but He is always at work. In hallways. With suitcases. Through a violin.

A time of mystery and unknowns

Autumn weather is unpredictable. The weather app tells you one thing, which is amusingly the opposite of the reality outside your window. Perhaps you've been caught off guard on an autumn's day – you leave your home in the morning without your rain jacket or umbrella due to some promising rays of sunshine, only to be caught in a downpour! Have you ever been in a season when you know you're doing the right thing and have made the right decision, yet things don't make complete sense? You can't see the whole picture, because the puzzle pieces are scattered on the table. Some have even fallen to the floor, and you can't find the lid of the puzzle box, which shows you the completed image. Welcome to the mystery. Welcome to the unknowns.

When autumn enters your inner world, bringing with it mystery and unknowns, be reminded of and reflect on this, dear reader:

God is still at work.

The Apostle Paul declares that 'we know that in all things God works for the good of those who love him, who have been called according to his purpose' (Romans 8:28). The wise King Solomon wrote: 'Trust in the Lord with all your heart and lean not on your own understanding; in all your ways submit to him, and he will make your paths straight' (Proverbs 3:5–6). You are not being called to be the detective with an assignment to solve the puzzles of your life. You are being called to place your trust in and follow after the One who is ordering your steps and accounting for your actions and circumstances. Calling first starts with, and is ultimately about, a trusting relationship with the One who has called you – what you get to 'do with your life' is the by-product. Knowing God is still at work in the midst of what we think is mysterious and filled with unknowns enables our soul to experience peace. After all, it's clearly not a mystery to the Lord, is it?

CHAPTER 3:

Love – Imperfectly Perfect

April 2009, Sydney, Autumn

Andrew's best man handed him his glasses when it was time for me to walk down the aisle. Andrew was in denial about the state of his short-sightedness, and when I heard Terry say, 'If you don't wear your glasses when she's walking down the aisle, you're not going to see all the details of how she looks. You only get that once.' I gave Andrew a look that said everything. *Wear the glasses*. Meanwhile, I was trying not to trip over in my new, ivory-white heels as I practised walking to the beat of *Pachelbel's Canon in D*. Nobody had warned us about how emotionally heightened wedding rehearsals are. Excitement, nervousness, panic, worry. Joy, stress, laughter, tears. Fumbling over words, trying to find the printed copies of the order of service, joining hands at the wrong moment. Confusion. Everyone snappy and tense. Adrenaline pumping. 'Better now than on the day,' said the minister calmly. David had seen all this carry-on before – the wise Anglican minister at All Saints' Church Woollahra had helped couples tie the knot for decades and he was about to do it once again for a twenty-seven-year-old woman and the twenty-nine-year-old man of her dreams.

* * *

The phrase 'it takes a village' usually refers to raising a child. I'm convinced it also applies to organising a wedding! Especially when you have only three months to plan it. Hilarious, really; we'd been on the phone confirming the number of guests to the caterers on the morning of our engagement party. Why only three months to plan a wedding? Andrew discovered that when you propose to a high school teacher, there's predestined windows of time to set the wedding date – school holidays. Proposing in December offered the April Easter holidays, the July mid-year winter holidays, the September spring holidays, or the end-of-school-year summer and Christmas holidays. I was already booked to return to Rwanda to volunteer at another teacher training conference, so that ruled out July. A year away seemed too long, as did September. Many couples prefer being engaged for a year or more – for a range of valid reasons. Andrew and I were not in that category. Both in our late twenties, we'd completed our education, had secure jobs and income, knew without a doubt that we wanted to spend the rest of our lives together, and just wanted to get on with it. So, an April wedding it would be.

With my family on the other side of the world, and Andrew's mum and siblings spread out over New South Wales – some a couple of hours' drive from Sydney – we watched the power of our village in action. Help, advice, generosity, encouragement and support flowed from lifelong friends, our church community, colleagues and from the unlikeliest of people, who seemed to cross our paths exactly when we needed them. You don't get to choose your biological family, but there are other families – villages, communities – you can choose to be a part of through intentionally reaching out, sharing life while breaking bread around the table, offering help one day, asking for it the next, allowing both tears and laughter to flow in their presence. God knows who you need long before you know it yourself. He can place you in a village, if you let Him. The village is sacred fellowship. Protection.

***

The silence was loud. Unspoken words hung in the air. We hadn't spoken much in a week. I shuffled in my chair and looked up as Andrew finally cleared his throat. *Here it comes*. I'd been preparing myself for his decision. And I was convinced I knew what it was. When Andrew and I started dating, he was offered the very thing he'd been working towards for most of his adult life. Having completed a Bachelor of Theology and served many years as a volunteer leader across different departments and ministries, his senior pastor had invited him to begin the process of ordination. *I'm going to be a pastor's wife*. Here's the catch – the pastor and the pastor's wife need to be at the same church. Makes sense. Here's the other catch – the soon-to-be ordained pastor and his soon-to-be wife attended different churches. And they both loved where they attended and volunteered. Probably why they hadn't had the conversation yet.

After a painful internal battle, I'd handed the decision over to Andrew to make. He could decide which church we'd make home for the rest of our engagement and as a newly married couple. I knew it needed to come from him. The theology of the marriage covenant and how it outworks itself practically is not the topic of this book, but releasing this specific decision to Andrew was a step of trust onto a whole new level of partnership. It was a defining moment in our relationship. Preservation.

I was gobsmacked. My mouth literally hung open in disbelief. I asked him to repeat himself. Poor guy. With tears in his eyes, Andrew took my hands in his. 'I'm not taking the ordination opportunity. I feel that God wants me to leave my church and join you at yours. I don't know if I'll ever be an ordained pastor, but when you're a pastor at heart, you can love people no matter where you are or what your title is.' *I'm not going to be a pastor's wife, after all.* Well, not in the way we thought. But that's usually the case in autumn.

* * *

'Where is he? Is he with you?' Kathy stood to her feet with outstretched arms, her heightened hearing compensating for her lack of sight. Kathy lived in a home in Denmark for people with severe physical and neurological disabilities. My parents were several hours away, in southern Sweden. Why were my parents and sister now living in the Nordics? Well, that becomes clearer later. Back to the moment my sister met my fiancé. I'd surprised Andrew with tickets to Copenhagen to meet my family during the Christmas of 2008. I also had a feeling he wanted to ask my dad a certain question before asking me one. I'm all for helping move a process along when needed. 'I'm right here, Kathy.' Andrew walked straight into her embrace. She never saw him with her eyes, but she saw him with her heart. 'He's a good one,' came the verdict, as she held him tightly. Tears silently streamed down our faces. Then she, as she often did, brought on the unexpected comic relief. 'Andrew's a sexy man!' Tears turned into laughter.

* * *

'Okay, it's now time.' Friday 17 April 2009. My flower girl, bridesmaid and matron of honour had reached the altar. My dad and I linked arms and took a deep breath as we made our appearance at the start of the aisle, *Pachelbel's Canon in D* reaching the peak of crescendo. My eyes locked with Andrew's. Yes, he was wearing his glasses. His best man had known best. Just as God knew best – that an imperfect city girl from Melbourne and an imperfect country boy from the Blue Mountains would be perfect for each other.

A time of preservation and protection

Both people and animals do specific things in autumn to preserve and protect life for the winter ahead. Animals in the wild gather and store food; some species prepare their hibernation spaces. Farmers work on their autumn harvest by collecting their reserve crops. Now, I'm neither an animal nor a farmer; however, I certainly start wearing more layers and thicker fabrics when autumn makes its appearance. We are also more aware of nutrition and boosting our immune systems in this lead-up to winter; health food stores fill with customers purchasing Vitamin D to combat the lack of sunshine and herbal teas to help keep colds away.

Our natural inclination in a season of change is to preserve and protect. During autumn seasons of the soul, it's important to build up your spiritual reserves and boost your spiritual health for the winter seasons inevitably on their way.

When autumn enters your inner world, stirring the need to preserve and protect, be reminded of and reflect on this, dear reader:

God knows what you need next.

Psalm 32:8 says: 'I will instruct you and teach you in the way you should go; I will counsel you with my loving eye on you.' You can trust that God will use your autumn season to nourish, strengthen and fortify your soul to withstand trials and tribulations that will come your way. Because they will come your way – Jesus makes this clear in John

16:33: 'I have told you these things, so that in me you may have peace. In this world you will have trouble. But take heart! I have overcome the world.'

God's instruction and counsel in Psalm 32 is coupled with love and care. God knows exactly what's ahead and, therefore, knows exactly what you need next. Will you ask Him to instruct you? Will you ask Him to show you what you need? Will you act on His counsel, even if it goes against your natural inclination? Will you trust the One who wants to protect and preserve you – the One who wants you to experience pure love?

CHAPTER 4:

Motherhood – Thirty and Pregnant

April 2011, Sydney, Autumn

It was everything we wanted it to be, and more. A joint thirtieth birthday party to celebrate this milestone age. We rented out a local coffee roastery – a popular café in Sydney's Hills District, in a trendy industrial space – and filled it with family and friends. Even though it was early autumn, the weather was still warm. Men were in short-sleeved shirts; women in strappy dresses. Delicious hot and cold finger foods, cocktails and mocktails, a dessert table laden with cupcakes, access to the coffee machine (latte, anyone?), heartfelt speeches by our husbands, music that got everyone on the dance floor, and thoughtful gifts.

It also marked twenty-five years of a friendship that has stood the test of time through every season. Claire and I first met in a church Sunday school when we were just five years old, and we've been friends ever since, both seeing each other through the best of times and the worst of times. She's a true sister – a lot of how my life has turned out thus far is because of her. 'That was *so* much fun!' I exclaimed, kicking off my black heels, trying to hide my swollen ankles so Andrew wouldn't start making a fuss – the doting father-to-be. I was four months pregnant with our first child, a daughter whom we couldn't wait to meet. Already a natural with babies, Andrew was filled with excitement. I, on the other hand, bottling up my fear of giving birth, had never changed a nappy throughout my first three decades and never gushed over a newborn baby. *What if I'm not a good mum?* I didn't dare voice my thoughts. Everyone was thrilled for me, for us.

* * *

Making a baby was fun; preparing for its entrance into the world was expensive. The first two years of our married life brought great change to our careers. Andrew bravely resigned from where he'd worked throughout most of his twenties, and accepted a new role at another institution that would provide a steep learning curve along with an increased salary and generous paternity leave package. I made the big step to shift out of classroom teaching and took on a role at regional level within New South Wales's education department, responsible for rolling out a new government initiative – a student service-learning programme – across all secondary schools across Western and Northern Sydney. It was a role that involved training teachers, implementing curriculum, managing budgets, presenting quarterly data-driven reports to politicians and, also, an increase in salary and generous maternity leave conditions. I can see now that while we thought this was all about God moving us forward in our careers, He was, in fact, paving the way of provision to welcome the third member of our family.

* * *

I have the propensity to be a control freak. Dreaded thoughts and worries about pregnancy problems, labour, birth, breastfeeding, changing nappies, sleep deprivation, post-birth recovery and keeping a completely helpless and vulnerable human being alive sent my fight-flight-freeze-or-fawn reactions into full throttle. At the back of my mind, I carried the fact that my mum, Evelyn Fitt, had almost died while giving birth to me in the May of 1981. Feeling like life was spinning out of control, I compensated by making as many Excel spreadsheets and to-do lists as possible. Hunched over my computer, typing away furiously, Andrew would simply raise an eyebrow and walk away. He knew when to just leave me be. But there was more going on. There always is, isn't there? We only see the tip of people's icebergs, unaware of what's lurking beneath. With my mum on the other side of the world, and my sister once so involved in my life and now severely sick, I felt uncertain and vulnerable.

Learning that a loss of control and letting go is the point at which God can reveal Himself as comforter – often through the words and actions of others – is a lesson that motherhood has taught, and continues to teach, me. Only four short months after our joint thirtieth, Claire threw me a fantastic baby shower. All my favourite savouries and sweets, beverages and hilarious games. Part way through the event, someone commented on the wide range of women present – different generations, cultures, beliefs, vocations and stages of life. I hadn't really noticed the diversity; this is what friendship had always looked like to me. I had learned over the years to find support and strength through my God-given sisterhood.

'Okay, there's one more speech,' Claire said. I looked on in confusion as she went and switched on the television in the lounge, where all the women had gathered for speeches and the opening of gifts. A short video began to play. My mum. She had recorded a speech for the baby shower. There wasn't a dry eye in the room by the time it had finished. I sensed the tangible presence of God's comfort, and I knew everything would be okay in one of the biggest transitions of my life – becoming a mother.

* * *

A sunny Tuesday at 14:33 in a Sydney hospital. The exact moment our daughter entered the world, her grand entrance already providing insight into the person she was, is and will be – her wide eyes taking it all in and a confident cry revealing the clear voice that would start saying her first words early. Annika, a Swedish name – a tribute to our shared love of Scandinavia and a feeling that we would one day live and work in that part of the world – meaning 'sweet-faced and highly favoured'. Her name inspired the song I intuitively started singing to settle her. *You're my little Annika, yes you are. You're my bright, shining star. I will always love you because you are my beautiful Annika, beautiful Annika.* 14:34. The birth of a mother, comforting her daughter.

A time of letting go and receiving comfort

The climax of autumn is when brown leaves fall to the ground, unable to cling to their branches. Flowers and plants wither and decay, returning to the muddy soil. The temperature rapidly plummets, the heat of summer only a distant memory. Death, loss, limitations, weaknesses, imperfections, failures and regrets. We would prefer not to process such pain. We ignore it. Avoid it. Deny it. Numb it. But autumn seasons of the soul don't allow us to do so – and for good reason.

You see, the pain of undealt-with pain eventually becomes more painful than the pain of dealing with the pain . . . read that again – slowly. *The pain of undealt-with pain eventually becomes more painful than the pain of dealing with the pain.* The Bible fortunately gives us permission to grieve and clearly shows us that being able to mourn and process suffering is a significant part of spiritual maturity and formation. We must 'be still before the Lord and wait patiently for him' (Psalm 37:7), knowing that 'unless a kernel of wheat falls to the ground and dies, it remains only a single seed. But if it dies, it produces many seeds' (John 12:24).

When autumn enters your inner world, bringing with it the reality of letting go, be reminded of, and reflect on this, dear reader:

God is your comforter.

> All praises belong to the God and Father of our Lord Jesus Christ. For he is the Father of tender mercy and the God of endless comfort. He always comes alongside us to comfort us in every suffering so that we can come alongside those who are in any painful trial. We can bring them this same comfort that God has poured out upon us. And just as we experience the abundance of Christ's own sufferings, even more of God's comfort will cascade upon us through our union with Christ.
>
> If troubles weigh us down, that just means that we will receive even more comfort to pass on to you for your deliverance! For the comfort pouring into us empowers us to bring comfort to you. And with this comfort upholding you, you can endure victoriously the same suffering that we experience. Now our hope for you is unshakable, because we know that just as you share in our sufferings you will also share in God's comforting strength.
>
> 2 Corinthians 1:3–7 TPT

The presence and the comfort of the Holy Spirit is needed in this season of letting go and surrendering to loss, especially in situations and areas of our lives in which true restoration cannot take place until we enter Heaven – where 'He will wipe every tear from their eyes, and there will be no more death or sorrow or crying or pain. All these things are gone forever' (Revelation 21:4 NLT).

PART I —

Cadence

A time of transition and change: God remains the same.
A time of mystery and unknowns: God is still at work.
A time of preservation and protection: God knows what you need next.
A time of letting go and receiving comfort: God is your comforter.

PART II —

Winter's Light

Allegro non molto
To tremble from cold in the icy snow,
In the harsh breath of a horrid wind;
To run, stamping one's feet every moment,
Our teeth chattering in the extreme cold.

Largo
Before the fire to pass peaceful,
Contented days while the rain outside pours down.

Allegro
We tread the icy path slowly and cautiously,
for fear of tripping and falling.
Then turn abruptly, slip, crash on the ground and,
rising, hasten on across the ice lest it cracks up.
We feel the chill north winds course through the home
despite the locked and bolted doors...
this is winter, which nonetheless
brings its own delights.[8]

PRELUDE –

Invitation

Winter – the season notorious for seasonal affective disorder (more commonly called the 'winter blues') when the dark and cold take their toll. During winter, we can find ourselves drifting into auto-pilot – survival mode – putting life on hold, waiting for the warmer months to arrive again. Winter seasons of the soul happen to us all and come in the forms of challenge, crisis, loneliness and heartbreak. Times when it seems like nothing is changing nor growing. Everything seems stagnant or dormant. However, we can welcome and embrace the winter seasons of the soul when we realise that winter plays a vital role in our spiritual, emotional and character development. Read these words penned by James in his New Testament epistle:

> James, a servant of God and of the Lord Jesus Christ,
> To the twelve tribes scattered among the nations:
> Greetings.
> Consider it pure joy, my brothers and sisters, whenever you face trials of many kinds, because you know that the testing of your faith produces perseverance. Let perseverance finish its work so that you may be mature and complete, not lacking anything.

James 1:1–4

Pure joy? Trials of many kinds? *Seriously?* Apparently so. I don't know about you, but I rarely feel joy in the middle of hardship. Quite the opposite, actually. But I get the feeling that James wasn't looking at his circumstances when he was in the middle of them. He was looking through them; he had a revelation that what he was *in* was developing a resilience that would get him *through*. And on the other side, he would have reached a new level of maturity and wholeness in Christ – not lacking anything. Dear reader, this happens to us in winter.

Here are four invitations that winter extends to us, which I believe will help you recognise and understand it when it arrives in your inner world:

1. An invitation to draw closer
2. An invitation to go deeper
3. An invitation to grow stronger
4. An invitation to shine brighter

Remember, this sacred season is about the process of learning in the dark how to be light.

All will be well. Just accept the invitations.

CHAPTER 5:

Grief and Healing – Rest and Recovery

December 2019, Copenhagen, Winter

'Off for a run?' asked my husband with an encouraging smile as he watched me reach for the neatly folded pile of running clothes in my wardrobe. It was 6:30 in the morning. The fact I was now getting up in the morning was a miracle in itself – the previous month of November had been mostly spent in bed. I'd used what little energy I had to be present with my children in the morning – pouring milk into bowls of cereal, searching for matching lids of snack containers, savouring hugs and kisses as they headed out the door – only to collapse back into bed in tears, needing to gain enough energy to do it all again when they got home – placing dinner plates on the table, coaxing little, freshly showered legs into stubborn pyjama bottoms, singing to sweet, drowsy-eyed faces as they drifted off to sleep, me following shortly after.

* * *

The weekly therapy sessions were the gift I didn't know I wanted. God always knows what we really need even when we don't. To think that He had gone ahead and made a way for these sessions to happen long before my crisis point came still moves me deeply. You see, I believe God can miraculously heal people in a moment. My dad had cancer when I was a little girl. The X-rays showed the tumours. Kathy and I prayed together for him every night before I went to bed, for many weeks. Possibly months. Then one day, the X-rays came back clear. Just like that. Cancer gone. Speechless doctors. But I also believe He brings healing through medical professionals, treatment and medication. I laugh at myself now when I think about my attitude during those initial therapy sessions. *Why do we need to talk about my childhood? I just want my hair to stop falling out. Just tell me what I need to do so I can get back to work and get on with my life.*

'A lot less *doing* and a lot more *being*, Celina,' was the wise response to the thoughts that clearly expressed themselves on my face. Being. Who would have thought that we need to learn to be? Turns out, I really needed to learn this lesson. I think we all do. To be still. To draw closer to our Healer.

* * *

Recovery requires surrender. It sounds romantic, doesn't it? It's not. Well, it wasn't for me, anyway. For me, surrender was tight-fisted, eyes squeezed shut, tears streaming down my face, back of my head against a wall one morning in November 2019. It was the defiant 'fine, have it your way!' of a child who knows when they've lost. Stripped of everything I had placed my identity in, I was now confronted with what remained. And I was horrified. Then, a still small voice: 'Celina, go for a run.' *Excuse me?* I blinked in disbelief. This was the response to my deflated and frustrated act of surrender? Celina. Go. For. A. Run. Five words. But that's all it takes, sometimes. Five words from the Lord can change your life.

Now, dear reader, you need to understand something. November in Denmark is the month of continual grey between eight in the morning and four in the afternoon, and black the rest of the time. Not the most ideal time to start running. Nonetheless, I searched for a pair of running shoes that I'd got for free from a colleague several years prior but hadn't yet used. I pulled on some exercise clothes, half amused, half freaked out. I walked out of the apartment building, took a deep breath and started to run. I arrived back to the front of the building ten minutes later, gasping for air. Some of my neighbours arrived at that moment, looking rather impressed – surely, I'd just completed a 12km run judging by the state of me. No. Just a lap around the block. 'Celina, do it again tomorrow.' Five more words.

* * *

Running became a sacred act. Holy ground. 'See you in a little while,' Andrew said as I headed out the door that December winter morning in 2019. My physical and spiritual practice had begun once again. If anyone had seen me running during that time, they would have seen my mouth moving. Saying something under my breath. *Probably talking to herself*, they would have thought. Yes. I was saying something to myself. I was repeating Proverbs 18:10 (NKJV) to be exact:

The name of the Lord is a strong tower; the righteous run to it and are safe. The name of the Lord is a strong tower; the righteous run to it and are safe. The name of the Lord is a strong tower; the righteous run to it and are safe.

Say His name.

Jehovah Jireh. My provider. Jehovah Rapha. My healer. Jehovah Shalom. My peace. Jehovah Jireh. My provider. Jehovah Rapha. My healer. Jehovah Shalom. My peace. Jehovah Jireh. My provider. Jehovah Rapha. My healer. Jehovah Shalom. My peace.

Words to the beat of my feet. Run. Say His name. Run. Say His name. Run. Say His name. Run. Say His name. Surrender draws you closer to the One who saves. Surrender leads you to the Strong Tower. And you can find safety there. You can find rest and recovery there.

An invitation to draw closer

One winter several years ago, when I was a teacher, I went out into the playground during break time and saw all the children huddled together, to keep warm. We do this instinctively, don't we? When it's cold, we draw close to sources of warmth – other people, a fireplace, a blanket, a steaming cup of coffee. But when we're going through a winter season of the soul – when things are hard, challenging and painful – we tend to do the opposite: we withdraw and isolate ourselves.

Why do we do that? Maybe it's because we're worried about what people will think about us and our circumstances. Perhaps it's pride: we want people to think we always have it together and don't like to admit struggles and weakness. Maybe it's independence: we want to stay in control and work things out for ourselves because we don't want to depend on someone else. God, however, wants us to draw closer. To

Him – the ultimate source of healing.

When winter enters your inner world, inviting you to draw closer, be encouraged to do this, dear reader:

Establish spiritual disciplines.

God is your source of warmth when your soul is facing winter. You need to draw closer, even when everything within you wants to stay away. James 4:8a says: 'Come near to God and he will come near to you.' How do we come near to God? There are many ways. Through the reading of the Word and the memorisation of Scripture – His voice needs to be louder than the voices of your circumstances. Through journaling your thoughts and expressing your feelings – pen marking paper, often joined by teardrops. Through sitting in silence and solitude – 'Solitude is a chosen separation for refining your soul. Isolation is what you crave when you neglect the first.'[9] Through a run in a forest as the sun is rising, a dip in the ocean in the middle of the day, a walk around the block as sunlight fades away and is replaced by moonlight – nothing like the splendour of creation to point you towards the Creator. Through music – singing songs of praise, playing instruments in worship, listening to sounds of both lament and anticipation. Through family and friends gathering around the table for a meal – breaking bread in remembrance of a broken body that replaced bondage with beauty.

> As the deer pants for streams of water,
> so my soul pants for you, my God.
> My soul thirsts for God, for the living God.
> When can I go and meet with God?
>
> Psalm 42:1–2

Navigating grief and finding healing involves discovering your way of drawing closer. We all do this differently, yet the core characteristics are the same: longing and intentionality. The former drives the latter; our hunger results in a plan. Our desperation draws us closer. And we are satisfied in His presence.

CHAPTER 6:

Calling – Packing for Rwanda

June 2008, Sydney, Winter

There were only a few weeks left to go. My left arm still sore from the final round of vaccinations, I pulled out my suitcase and stared into my wardrobe. Two weeks in Kigali, Rwanda, volunteering at a teacher training conference for a faith-based non-profit. Hundreds of Rwandan educators would be attending, and I had the honour of presenting a series of workshops to both help upskill the participants in the English language and equip them with pedagogical practices to engage their students in literacy lessons. I loved the concept and approach the organisation had – annual professional development conferences for the teachers, who would then bring their learning back into the classroom to benefit their students, rather than our teams going into the classroom to be guest teachers and giving the children a momentary memorable experience as opposed to lasting impact. If there was anything I'd learned from a double bachelor's degree in arts and education, a master's degree specialising in international education, plus three and a half years of teaching experience under my belt as a teacher, it was this: education changes directions, and a teacher's words shape futures. And it all begins with connection – people will want to learn from you if they know you genuinely like and care about them.

* * *

'Do you want to be a part of it, Celina?' my friend asked me. Sarah and her husband, Paul, had just finished telling me about a weekly Bible study course they were going to start running for a small group in their home. Based on the book, *The Purpose Driven Life*,[10] the curriculum was designed to help people discover their purpose, ignite dreams, make goals, and draw closer to their Creator. I was almost twenty-three years old and had nearly finished my first year as a full-time music and English secondary school teacher at a government school in Melbourne's south-eastern suburbs. That entire year of 2005 was a baptism of fire. Nothing prepares you for standing in front of twenty-eight teenagers – who are not there by choice – and attempting to 'enlighten' them until, well, you're standing in front of them, realising that the odds were never in your favour to begin with.

'Yes, I'd like to be a part of it! Thanks for asking me,' I replied. The truth is, I was lonely. Ironic, isn't it? Surrounded by hundreds of people in my workplace – students, colleagues, parents – having many great friends through local church communities and living with my sister and brother-in-law, and yet waking up each morning with a sharp stab of phantom pain. I've discovered that it's not just a physical phenomenon – feeling pain from a part of the body that's no longer there – but also an ache in the deepest part of your soul that you left behind at Copenhagen Airport when you said goodbye to your parents and moved back to the other side of the world, wondering if you'd ever live in the same country again. Why were my parents in Denmark at that point in my life? We'll get to that soon.

* * *

My academic hat, a little too big, kept sliding to one side as I stood by the side of the stage waiting for my name to be announced. After three years of coursework and writing my thesis, while working as a full-time teacher, I graduated with a master's of education. Enrolling in this postgraduate programme was the result of participating in that Bible study course several years earlier. It was a defining time – six weekly sessions of teaching that both confronted me and stirred up an excitement I hadn't felt for a while; honest and encouraging group discussions with people, most of whom I'd never met before yet welcomed me and genuinely wanted to get to know me; and the God-whisper I sensed during a time of prayer at the end of one of the sessions. 'Celina, do a master's degree.' Five words.

My favourite professor read out my name and gave me a proud smile. The audience applauded as I walked across the stage to accept my certificate. Even though I felt great happiness and relief, there was a niggling sense of unease and confusion that I couldn't put to rest. I sat back down again and looked at the certificate on my lap – beautiful calligraphy and the red wax seal – and read the phrase 'specialising in international education'. When I'd filled in my application form and chosen my pathway, I'd planned to tick the box that said 'education leadership' – a pathway for teachers aspiring to become, for example, school principals. But as I lifted my black-ink pen, I couldn't bring myself to tick that box. Another box caught my eye, drawing me to it like a magnet. International education. It didn't make sense to me – not when I applied, not when I pored over the readings and wrote the assignments, not when I graduated, not when I held the certificate in my hands.

* * *

'Next up, we have Celina,' my youth pastor announced, gesturing for me to come up on stage. It was my turn. It had taken a lot of coaxing to finally convince me to do this. Butterflies fluttered in my stomach and my pulse suggested I was sprinting. I wasn't. I was standing stone still – a microphone in one hand and my Bible in the other. You would have thought that many years of playing the violin in front of thousands of people would have prepared this sixteen-year-old for sharing a three-minute encouragement in front of a church youth group of fifty people. It hadn't. My Bible was obviously smaller than my violin, but it felt bigger in my hand. Weightier. Defining.

'Praise be to the God and Father of our Lord Jesus Christ, the Father of compassion and the God of all comfort, who comforts us in all our troubles, so that we can comfort those in any trouble with the comfort we ourselves receive from God,' I said, my voice shaking slightly. 'For just as we share abundantly in the sufferings of Christ, so also our comfort abounds through Christ. If we are distressed, it is for your comfort and salvation; if we are comforted, it is for your comfort, which produces in you patient endurance of the same sufferings we suffer.' My voice stopped shaking. 'And our hope for you is firm, because we know that just as you share in our sufferings, so also you share in our comfort.' I spent my remaining time explaining this passage, which I had just read out from 2 Corinthians 1:3–7. At the end, I hesitantly offered to pray for anyone needing comfort from Jesus. A sea of raised hands filled the room. Many people cried. I was stunned. So was my youth pastor. I don't think God was.

* * *

Laughter filled the dirt-floored classroom. Have you ever been in the presence of contagious joy? I certainly didn't expect to find it there. Typical, right? We look for the places where we think Joy would most likely hang out. But Joy dwells within and comes along with us. If we don't find Joy in our circumstances, it's because Joy's not within. That's what my workshop group of almost thirty Rwandan teachers taught me – a lesson more valuable than anything I tried to teach them.

Back to their laughter. I mean, who wouldn't be entertained by an Aussie girl in her mid-twenties attempting to pick up heavy bricks, which she'd dragged from outside, and put them on a table at the front of the room? We were several days into the teacher training conference, and the topic for that afternoon's English workshop was text analysis. I know. Sounds riveting, doesn't it? It was also the graveyard shift – straight after lunch, during the hottest part of the day. Text analysis and I didn't stand much of a chance. Until inspiration hit when I looked out the unglazed window and spotted them. The pile of bricks.

'Think of text as a wall made of bricks,' I began, trying to hold one up in my dirty hands. The teachers leaned forward. 'Each brick plays its part in that wall. Each brick is a word, set in place with the cement of literary devices. When an author writes text, they're constructing the wall with their bricks and cement – their words and literary devices. And the wall has an impact on the person it surrounds.' The teachers were now nodding and carefully watching me stack bricks. 'We need to teach our students to pull apart the wall – to deconstruct the text – to examine each word, identify the literary devices, understand how they contribute to the overall text, and the impact on the reader.'

The teachers erupted into lively discussions with their peers, the heat of the day now forgotten. I sat down with one group and listened to their conversation. Sitting in the presence of their genuine gladness despite hardship, their overflowing gratitude despite lack, their generous embrace despite pain, and their gentle understanding despite challenge poured much-needed water over my dehydrated soul. I'd packed my bags for Rwanda to help educators teach English. Turns out I'd packed my bags for Rwanda so teachers could help me breathe. And the Lord knew I needed it, because little did I know that on my way home, via Jomo Kenyatta International Airport, I was going to receive a phone call that would turn my world upside down, causing me to change my flight so I could get to my sister as soon as possible. To Kathy, who would be in an intensive care unit in a Danish hospital. In a coma that would tragically change her life – and her family's lives – forever.

An invitation to go deeper

There's something so beautiful and special about a 'white Christmas' in the Northern Hemisphere. Because it's so cold, it's all about opening your home and inviting people to celebrate and connect. Christmastime during the COVID-19 pandemic was difficult for so many. Families and friends were unable to gather in the ways they're used to due to lockdowns and restrictions.

Winter seasons of the soul can feel lonely and confronting. We often think nobody else understands what we're going through. It's a lie the enemy would love you to believe to prevent you from experiencing something that actually helps during winter – fellowship. We were not created to live this life on our own. After creating Adam, our Creator made Eve, saying, 'It's not good for the Man to be alone; I'll make him a helper, a companion' (Genesis 2:18 MSG).

When winter enters your inner world, inviting you to go deeper, be encouraged to do this, dear reader:

Deepen relationships.

Romans 12:15 tells us to 'rejoice with those who rejoice; mourn with those who mourn'. Allow people to see you as you really are in this season – not just your strengths, but also your weaknesses. There is power in experiencing fellowship, when people don't just rejoice with you in the good times but mourn with you in the bad times. This requires courage because vulnerability is difficult and humbling and . . . vital.

> Two are better than one because they have a more satisfying return for their labor; for if either of them falls, the one will lift up his companion. But woe to him who is alone when he falls and does not have another to lift him up.
>
> Ecclesiastes 4:9–10 AMP

The more we mature in our spirituality, the more we understand that while 'the gifts and the calling of God are irrevocable' (Romans 11:29 NKJV), He uses others to both stir up and bring forth our calling. Relationships must be bravely embraced and willingly deepened.

CHAPTER 7:

Love – 'What Guy Would Ever Marry You?'

June 1994, Melbourne, Winter

'Sticks and stones may break my bones, but names will never hurt me.' Did you ever hear that growing up? Or some variation of it, perhaps? What a load of rubbish. I don't know about you, but I'd rather have had broken bones than some of the words said to me throughout my life. Especially during my teenage years. Fortunately, Mrs McNamara also thought that saying was rubbish. Early thirties (that seemed ancient to a thirteen-year-old), wavy, chocolate-brown hair, very cool glasses framing kind eyes. She was the school counsellor, and I had become a regular visitor, after being referred by an observant teacher who had picked up on the bullying. 'I don't know what I did wrong. What's wrong with *me*? Why is everyone picking on *me*?' My second year of secondary school was turning into a nightmare. Mrs McNamara handed me another tissue. Have you ever asked a question from a place of deep despair, only to receive a response in the form of another question? Counsellors, therapists, psychologists, psychiatrists, social workers, Jesus ('Do you want to be made well?').[11] All excellent at it. 'What if you *haven't* done anything wrong, Celina? What if there's nothing wrong with *you*? What if this says more about *them*?' I blew my nose again. I just wanted *them* to stop.

* * *

My primary school teachers kept telling my parents I'd do well at secondary school. I was a topic of great pride, having been accepted into Caulfield Grammar School – a private Anglican school in a wealthy part of Melbourne – which required passing vigorous entrance exams and an interview with the headmaster. My parents sacrificed so much to pay the fees for this school known for its academic results and passionate commitment to the arts. I would later be granted an academic and a music scholarship for the second half of my time there, which relieved some of the financial pressure. My violin playing and creative writing skills paved a way for me – I eventually became first chair violinist (the concertmaster) for the school's esteemed orchestra and submitted articles for the school's publications.

But. There's always a but in these situations. There was a lot of pressure to succeed, and competition was fierce. I didn't mind though; I loved learning, loved my teachers, loved the extra-curricular opportunities, and I made some good friends in my first year. And friendships are key at that stage in life. You can, therefore, imagine the distress, confusion and fear that engulfed me the morning I turned up at school, went to my locker and greeted my girlfriends as per usual, only for them to smirk, turn their backs on me and walk away laughing. Stunned, I avoided eye contact with those who'd witnessed the embarrassing scene and walked head down to the first class of the day.

This went on for days. Weeks. Months. Others joined in. Even the boys. Exclusion. Whispers behind my back. Rumours. Jokes about the fact my dad was a church minister. We were at an Anglican school for crying out loud – what on earth was the big deal about that?! No more invitations to birthday parties. Escaping to the toilets or the library during breaks. Faking being sick so I could stay at home for a break from it all. I stopped putting my hand up in class. Instead, I put on invisible armour and wore it to school each day – *don't stand out, keep out of their way, keep your mouth shut, don't make it worse.* The battle plan was clear: dodge the bullets, dodge the words. What wasn't clear was for how long I'd have to endure the anguish of rejection for reasons unknown to me.

* * *

Deafening silence. Followed by thunderous applause. It caught me off guard. Taking the hand of each person to my side, I took my bow. The applause kept on going. I bowed again, catching sight of my family, who were cheering loudly. Side of stage, clapping proudly, was my English teacher, who was also the director of my school's lower-secondary musical, *Calamity Jane*. It was a year later. 1995.

'Why don't you try out for the musical?' Mrs McNamara asked. I misunderstood. 'Oh, I'll probably be playing my violin.' She shook her head. 'No, I mean, why don't you try out for one of the acting parts?' There are always moments when you doubt your counsellor and think they've seriously lost the plot. This was one of those moments. *An acting part?! That's the last thing I want to do!*

After almost a year, the bullying had come to an end. A combination of teacher intervention and my dad calling the father of one of the main instigators. Horrifying for a teen, yet admittedly helpful. Despite the daily onslaught ceasing, it would be a long journey to recover from the ordeal. I had become timid, shy, uncertain, fearful, constantly on high alert – the total opposite of the confident little girl I once was. Kathy sadly watched her little sister's bright spark slowly snuff out, no matter how hard she comforted and encouraged me.

'Celina, thanks for waiting!' The director handed me a script. 'Let's read a scene together.' To be honest, what happened next is a blur. Months later, I would learn that the teachers in the room abruptly stopped what they were doing at the sound of a girl's voice reading out the lines of a script she'd never laid eyes on until that moment. I would later learn that they hadn't seen it coming. I would later learn that the girl who had spent almost a year hiding in the shadows was destined for the stage. And not just for her violin playing. I would later learn that I'd got a part. *The* part. Calamity Jane. The very thing I was avoiding the most was the very thing that recovered my voice – allowing myself to be seen. *I just blew in from the windy city; the windy city is mighty pretty; but they ain't got what we got, no siree.*[12]

* * *

Another break-up. More heartache. Solace found in the next relationship. Repeat. Not the best merry-go-round to be on, but like all on rides that just go round and round, you really just need to step off and find a new ride that's actually going somewhere. 'I don't understand why you keep getting involved with guys that aren't good for you.' My university friend was a combination of blunt honesty and sensitive compassion. 'Well, I'm never going to get married, so does it even matter?' The words rushed out before my brain could stop them. I stared at my friend in horror. She stared back, both shocked and unsurprised. Other words came flooding back. *What guy would ever marry you?* The taunts, the laughter, the sheer cruelty of it all. Then, a revelation. Here I was, at the start of my twenties, and words from my early teens were shaping my life as an adult – I was continually changing who I was to fit in, seeking approval and acceptance through hiding the real me, and getting involved in relationships that just confirmed what I didn't know I believed. 'Sounds like you have a few issues to sort out,' my friend said dryly, before taking a sip of her flat white. The university student café served great coffee. We both laughed hysterically.

* * *

'It's hard, but you can only control your own choices,' Mrs McNamara said softly. 'People change, circumstances change, and you will change, too. Things don't stay the same forever. The bullying won't last forever. You need to choose how you're going to respond.' I was ready to hear that then. Deep down, I think I already understood that this terrible time of my life was training for the future. My dad had once woken up at 5am every day for several weeks, to join me for my daily violin practice downstairs and help me master my major and minor scales. He'd pull a slip of paper out of a small box. 'D major, three octaves, slurred.' 'G harmonic minor, two octaves, detached.' Over and over and over again. Ascending and descending, my dexterity improving over time. Fingers forming new and needed calluses. Resilience, endurance, patience. The foundation of being able to play pieces of music that would sound effortless to the audience, while only a few would witness the invitation to keep growing stronger, even when it hurt.

An invitation to grow stronger

It can be a steep learning curve for tourists and immigrants figuring out the different types of outdoor clothing they need for facing the harsh elements of a Scandinavian winter. In Denmark, there's a saying that goes like this: 'There's no such thing as bad weather, just the wrong clothing!'[13] In other words, if you have the right jackets, snowsuits, waterproof boots, gloves, scarves and hats, you really should be able to get on with your life as per normal regardless of what's happening outdoors. Technically speaking, of course.

Times of challenge, crisis, hardship and pain can feel so harsh, can't they? Your soul gets battered by stormy winds, torrential rain and freezing temperatures all at once. It's not fun at all! But just as you can choose the right clothing to suit the weather, you can make the right choices to withstand the winter seasons that your inner world faces. This may be hard to read, but while we tend to focus more on external circumstances, God is focused on what's happening on the inside. He wants us to grow stronger.

When winter enters your inner world, inviting you to grow stronger, be encouraged to do this, dear reader:

Persevere through challenge and wait patiently for change.

The Apostle Paul, having endured shipwreck, beatings, imprisonment, court trials and abandonment throughout his ministry years, was able to proclaim:

> We also rejoice in our sufferings, because we know that suffering produces perseverance; perseverance, character; and character, hope.
>
> Romans 5:3–4

Suffering. Perseverance. Character. Hope. Repeat. And as you patiently wait for change, remember:

> Since we are surrounded by such a great cloud of witnesses, let us throw off everything that hinders and the sin that so easily entangles, and let us run with perseverance the race marked out for us.
>
> Hebrews 12:1

There are some things the stormy winds need to blow out of our inner world for us to recognise, and experience, love the way God intended. But take heart – torrential rains cease. Temperatures warm up again. Keep on going. Allow your character to be strengthened. 'Relax, everything's going to be all right; rest, everything's coming together; open your hearts, love is on the way!' (Jude 1:2 MSG).

CHAPTER 8:

Motherhood – Maternity Leave for the Second Time

February 2016, Copenhagen, Winter

Our family expanded from three to four unique human beings four years after Annika's birth. Arriving shortly after midnight in a Copenhagen hospital, our son, Frederik, made a calm and relaxed entrance. We chose the Danish spelling – a royal name meaning 'peaceful ruler'. I knew right away this boy would be known for his influence and generous, tender-hearted nature. Both children were born on the thirteenth of their respective months – one arriving a week 'early' in Sydney in 2011, the other a week 'late' in Copenhagen in 2015. I became pregnant with one child within a month of 'trying', and pregnant with the other after eighteen months of challenge. Both pregnancies were smooth, yet there was concern in one pregnancy that the baby might be born with a permanent disability. We declined the medical advice to terminate in the early weeks of the first trimester – prepared to accept what would be, would be. And how overjoyed we were when the declaration of 'a totally healthy baby!' was made moments after birth. I enjoyed a spinal epidural during one delivery and the help of 'gas' (Entonox) during the other. In fact, when contractions were at their peak, I may have said I wanted to leave Andrew and marry the gas, much to his and the midwives' amusement. Overall, they were both such positive and profound experiences despite such different cultural philosophies and practices between Australia and Denmark regarding labour and birth. Why were we living in Denmark? You got it – more on that later.

* * *

When it comes to maternity leave, the Danish welfare system knows what it's doing. With a combination of full-time salary from the school I worked at, along with government benefits towards the end, I was able to be at home with Frederik for a full year with pay. Remarkable. I am thankful to this day. While maternity leave with Annika in Sydney involved preparing to move country, maternity leave with Frederik in Copenhagen involved trying to establish ourselves in our new home country. Winter was especially cold that year, and I can now see I'd been suffering from post-natal blues during the first couple of months. Fast forward two years. The rental lease on our apartment was coming to an end, and Andrew was made redundant from his first full-time job in Copenhagen after a temporary contract at another organisation expired. One of my heart's desires was to remain in the same neighbourhood, but that was beginning to seem like it would never happen. But we'd been through worse. 'Look how far we've come,' Andrew reminded me one evening, when we were both desperately trying to get our children to sleep. 'We need to remember all the miracles we experienced during our first couple of years here. If God did those things back then, He can most definitely do those things again!' Forever the optimist, my love.

* * *

Their eyes filled with tears. A moment of silence. Then, 'Your story is so inspiring. Thank you for telling us. It's given us hope.' Andrew and I had just finished sharing how God came through for our family during the early years of Frederik's life. Our friends were going through the same thing – uncertainty surrounding accommodation, unemployment, and sheer exhaustion.

Andrew's redundancy had been a blessing in disguise. With three months' salary paid out in full, he was able to invest his time and energy into finding us a new place to live. 'I have an idea!' he declared one afternoon in May 2018. He'd started packing boxes again. With one month to go until we had to move out, I was becoming more stressed by the hour. His idea? Sticking up posters around our apartment complex that featured a family photo and a message in both English and Danish explaining how we needed a new apartment as soon as possible. 'What do you think?' I was speechless. Not in a good way. Mortified.

A *photo* on a *poster*? But I had no other ideas left. Andrew got on with making the posters, knowing better than to involve me in choosing the photo. It was a Monday evening.

There was a knock on our door on the Wednesday morning. Neither of us expecting guests, I curiously made my way down the hallway to open the door. An elderly woman in the apartment complex handed me a piece of paper. 'I saw your poster yesterday,' she began. 'I then had coffee with my friend, who lives in a building that has an empty apartment that's being renovated.' I looked at the piece of paper. A name and a phone number. 'That's the owner,' she went on to explain. 'Perhaps give him a call.' Too stunned to ask her where the mystery apartment even was, I thanked her and handed the note to Andrew without saying a word. He didn't say anything either. He didn't need to; his grin said it all. *The poster was a good idea, hey?*

Andrew managed to get hold of the owner by the Thursday evening. It 'just so happened' the apartment would be available in a few more weeks – the exact time we needed it. It 'just so happened' the owner hadn't advertised it yet. It 'just so happened' he would be at the apartment the next day. 'Would you like to come and see it?' he asked Andrew. And it 'just so happened' God cared about the deep desires of our hearts: the apartment was in the same neighbourhood – right across the street from where we were living to be exact – and the layout was almost identical. I finally admitted the poster had been a good idea.

Have you ever closely lined up dominoes and pushed the first one into the next? Children love watching what we know to be the domino effect – and in life, it's when one thing leads to another, causing everything to fall into place. By the following week, we had signed the rental contract for the apartment across the road. An unlimited time agreement. We no longer needed to wonder what would happen at the end of each year. In that same week, Andrew received a phone call from a company asking him to come in for a conversation about a job. Turns out that someone who worked there knew Andrew and had put his name forward. That conversation led to a job offer, a successful salary negotiation and a signed contract within forty-eight hours. And as to how we managed to furnish our new apartment (our first apartment had come fully furnished), it 'just so happened' a friend of ours called, whose father was the manager of a hotel that had recently been refurnished. He wondered whether we'd be interested in any of the furniture before it got donated to charity. A couch, armchairs, cabinets, shelves, artwork, lamps, a desk and rugs were carried into our new apartment on the day we moved in. The warm weather had arrived once again. Darkness had made the miracle all the more brighter and brought much-needed hope.

An invitation to shine brighter

Evening walks during winter, especially in a city, are a beautiful experience. Many Danes don't close their curtains in the evening. The warm glow of lamps, candles on windowsills and pendants hanging from ceilings, combined with evenly spaced streetlamps, light up the black night. Signs of life coming from other houses, apartments and buildings are a reminder that people are carrying on regardless of the winter's night.

Winter seasons of the soul can feel terribly dark at times, can't they? When you go through a tough time in an area of your life, it can easily seem like you're in no position to help others. *What do I have to offer? I'm a mess! How could I help them when I'm in such a hard place myself? They wouldn't want my help anyway – they know what I'm going through.* Familiar? It's okay. We've all thought those thoughts at one point or another. Contrary to how you feel, I want you to know that even when you find yourself in a winter season on the inside, you can still be a shining light for someone else.

When winter enters your inner world, inviting you to shine brighter, be encouraged to do this, dear reader:

Bring hope to others.

Take these words of Jesus to heart:

> "Your lives light up the world. Let others see your light from a distance, for how can you hide a city that stands on a hilltop? And who would light a lamp and then hide it in an obscure place? Instead, it's placed where everyone in the house can benefit from its light. So don't hide your light! Let it shine brightly before others, so that the commendable

> things you do will shine as light upon them, and then they will give their praise to your Father in heaven."
>
> Matthew 5:14–16 TPT

What brings hope isn't watching people live a perfect life, but watching them live an imperfect life while trusting in a perfect God. That's what causes people to ask, 'What's different about you? How can you still have joy even though you're going through such pain right now? Why are you still able to keep on going when most people would have given up by now?'

Shine in the darkness. Your winter season will encourage someone else. It's not all in vain. Bright-white snow that falls during the night lights up a dark winter's morning. And winter will come to an end at the right time; the story you'll have at the end of this season will be a bright shining light that allows others to see Jesus.

PART II –

Cadence

An invitation to draw closer: establish spiritual disciplines.
An invitation to go deeper: deepen relationships.
An invitation to grow stronger: persevere through challenge and wait patiently for change.
An invitation to shine brighter: bring hope to others.

PART III —

Spring’s Hope

Allegro
Springtime is upon us.
The birds celebrate her return with festive song,
and murmuring streams are
softly caressed by the breezes.
Thunderstorms, those heralds of Spring, roar,
casting their dark mantle over heaven.
Then they die away to silence,
and the birds take up their charming songs once more.

Largo
On the flower-strewn meadow, with leafy branches
rustling overhead, the goat-herd sleeps,
his faithful dog beside him.

Allegro
Led by the festive sound of rustic bagpipes,
nymphs and shepherds lightly dance
beneath the brilliant canopy of spring.[14]

PRELUDE –

Decision

In the Northern Hemisphere, the month of March is a welcome relief from the dark and cold months of winter. In the Southern Hemisphere, it's September. The memory of winter starts to fade when spring appears. The intangible weight that's been on our shoulders for months begins to lift. As we stretch post-slumber, half yawning, and look around, we see things afresh. Something has shifted. Something has changed. Is it you? Is it your circumstances? Is it both?

When we feel that shift, decisions need to be made. And not just minor decisions – *what should I have for lunch today?* – major decisions: the I'm-standing-at-the-crossroads-and-need-to-pick-which-way types of decisions. One section of Moses's final address to the Israelites before commissioning Joshua is about the decision to follow God or to reject Him.

> This day I call the heavens and the earth as witnesses against you that I have set before you life and death, blessings and curses. Now choose life, so that you and your children may live and that you may love the LORD your God, listen to his voice, and hold fast to him. For the LORD is your life, and he will give you many years in the land he swore to give to your fathers, Abraham, Isaac and Jacob.
>
> Deuteronomy 30:19–20

It's dramatic reading from a historical narrative perspective. And it should have an impact on us indeed. These words should move us and guide us daily. Aren't all our decisions either moving us towards the Lord or away from Him? Towards life. Towards death. Towards blessings. Towards curses.

Here are four decisions that spring asks you to make, which I believe will help you recognise and understand spring when it arrives in your inner world:

1. A decision to take steps of faith
2. A decision to make plans to bless
3. A decision to allow space to simplify
4. A decision to look ahead with expectation

Remember, this sacred season is about holding onto the promises of hope.

All will be well. Just make the decisions.

CHAPTER 9:

Grief and Healing – A Resignation Letter and a Pandemic

April 2020, Copenhagen, Spring

Intellectual symptoms first. Forgetfulness, inability to problem solve or make decisions, decreased attention span. Emotional symptoms second. Lack of motivation, no more laughter, crying multiple times a day. Physical symptoms finally. Inevitably. Lethargy, headaches, loss of appetite. The pathway to crisis. A three-stage plan. But we don't even know it until – well, until we know it, I guess. But here's the miracle: the pathway to crisis can become the pathway to transformation. With the help of my psychiatrist, I retraced my steps. Years and years and years of steps. The brain absorbs it all, creating countless pathways as a result. It's those pathways we need to learn and care more about.

Along with therapy, I started taking care of my body – movement, sleep, water, food intake, vitamin supplements. My old friends, Productivity and Accomplishment, battled it out with my new friends, Silence and Solitude. They introduced me to Vulnerability. It turned out people like me better without a mask on. I filled up several journals, many pages stained with tears. Read books and listened to podcasts on contemplative spiritual practices. Wept through guided prayer exercises and gasped in astonishment during the Prayer of Examen when the Holy Spirit showed me where He had been at work in my life that day.

When it all fell apart. Interestingly, my Bible then started falling apart. Like, literally. The covers became unglued to the spine from being handled so much in a short period. I still refuse to fix it or use a new one when I preach – it serves as a powerful reminder. It keeps me humble. We are only ever a step away from heading back to crisis if we don't hang on tightly to His words. To the Way.

* * *

'Celina, you no longer have depression. I'm officially clearing you of the diagnosis. Let's now meet every second week for a bit, then perhaps monthly?' Mid-January 2020. What a way to start the year! Healing happens in reverse. Physical symptoms first. My hair stopped falling out, the knot in my chest subsided, and I was sleeping better. Emotional symptoms second. The look of shock and delight on my children's faces when I burst into laughter over Christmas. Had it really been that long since they'd heard their mum laugh? Intellectual symptoms finally. Inevitably. I stopped asking Andrew where my keys were and had opinions again.

I was twenty minutes early for my appointment that morning when my psychiatrist gave me the good news. Her office was in the heart of Copenhagen, next to a castle and a vast public garden. I went for a little walk to pass the time. I turned a corner along the gravel-stone path, then came to an abrupt stop. The smallest fragment of sunlight was piercing through the cloud, enough to light up the sky and create a pale patch of blue in the middle of the grey. I grinned. And I felt joy bubble up inside of me. It was a physical, emotional and mental experience. And it was profoundly spiritual. Divine healing. The hard work of recovery met by the healing touch of the hand of God.

It's important for me to emphasise that while I was cleared of my diagnosis within four months, it would be a couple more years until I truly understood my limits, made Sabbath holy in my life and, after much trial and error, discovered the routines, rhythms and activities that keep me grounded, healthy and refreshed. Recovery is not linear. It takes you up and down, backwards and forwards – yet, when you look back, you see the progress.

* * *

You would've thought that I'd have been thrilled. Yes. And no. Thrilled as I celebrated the victory with my nearest and dearest – tears of gratitude and joy, words of praise to Jehovah Rapha. The Lord heals. Not so thrilled at starting my entry plan back into the workplace. Back to normal, right? Back to how things used to be. But what happens when you're no longer the same person? Well, you start to take new steps. But that requires a new vision. In the September of 2013, I had set up a business. The reason I did this was so that I could proofread some academic papers and be able to invoice and accept payment in accordance with the Danish tax rules. As the years went on, I took on small editing projects here and there – creative projects that energised me. A few months before the day it all fell apart, I had turned down an incredible writing opportunity because it required full-time focus. *Oh well, some things are just not meant to be*. Perhaps.

* * *

Andrew turned forty in the spring of 2020. Unlike the big celebration we had thought it would be in that April, it was a small event. Us and our children. Why? We were in lockdown due to the COVID-19 pandemic. I stood in the kitchen, lighting the candles on his birthday cake. I caught sight of the branches moving gently in the breeze just outside the window. If you looked close enough, you could see little bumps of green – new life tentatively making its anticipated appearance. New beginnings.

Andrew blew out the candles, placed cake onto plates and smiled at me. We exchanged a knowing look that reflected the uncertainty and nervousness we were both feeling. His fortieth birthday also marked the first day of me working full-time in my business without any income from my previous job. I'd handed in my resignation letter on the last business day of February 2020, giving the required one-month notice. It was a bittersweet day, that's for sure! After almost two decades as a teacher – at the age of thirty-eight – I made a career change. A step of faith towards a new dream birthed from crisis.

Then the world shut down.

* * *

God! A pandemic?! You knew this was coming. Why would you then lead me to leave my secure job and go into my business full-time?

Celina, you needed to resign in February because you would have been too scared to do it now.

And the incredible writing project I'd turned down? Well, it came back to me – my first project beginning a new season as a full-time editor, ghostwriter and book coach. That's what happens. He takes nightmares and turns them into dreams that lead you into spring.

A decision to take steps of faith

The start of spring is often characterised by rain. For people living in cities, spring rain can be annoying. But for a farmer, whose livelihood is the farm, spring rain is a blessing! You see, when the spring rain comes, seeds intentionally planted in the ground begin to germinate, resulting in the first signs of plant shoots and flowers poking through the soil. However, for any of this to work, the seeds need to be there – in position, ready for the rain – in the first place.

In the same way, spring seasons of your inner world can be seasons when your ideas, dreams, goals and hard work begin to blossom into something beautiful. When opportunity and divine connections shower down, upon which seeds of your planting will they fall? Are you ready for the rain?

When spring enters your inner world, asking you to take steps of faith, be encouraged to do this, dear reader:

Bravely act on your dreams.

It's a decision to see your dreams become a reality and to do the hard work. While calling is from the Lord, we are not called to sit back and do nothing and wait for Him to do everything. And while He could (He is God, after all!), He involves us in the process. We can choose whether to participate. Habakkuk, a prophet in the Old Testament, was discouraged by all he saw happening around him. In response to his confusion and questioning, God redirected him to vision and to patience.

> And then GOD answered: "Write this. Write what you see. Write it out in big block letters so that it can be read on the run. This vision-message is a witness pointing to what's coming. It aches for the coming—it can hardly wait! And it doesn't lie. If it seems slow in coming, wait. It's on its way. It will come right on time."
>
> Habakkuk 2:2–3 MSG

Additionally, the book of Proverbs is filled with straightforward advice that you can action today:

> Work hard at your job and you'll have what you need . . . hard work brings blessings back to you . . . If you work hard at what you do, great abundance will come to you.
>
> Proverbs 12:11a, 14b; 14:23a TPT

Ploughing the soil and planting seeds requires vision, hard work and patience. However, when the rain comes – and it will come – you will begin to see the fruit of your labour. As you take steps of faith, God blesses and provides.

CHAPTER 10:

Calling – One-Way Ticket to Denmark

September 2012, Sydney, Spring

'Happy birthday to Annika, happy birthday to you!' Andrew and I, proud parents, helped our one-year-old daughter blow out the candle on her birthday cake as family and friends cheered and clapped. First birthday parties are a big deal – more for the parents than for the oblivious child. In our case, however, Annika was oblivious to so much more – that the birthday present she had received was a ticket to the other side of the world. And it was one-way.

* * *

Finish school. Get a degree in something useful. Get a job. Fall in love. Get engaged. Get married. Buy a house. Don't forget the white-picket fence. Have a child. Then have some more. Sell the first house. Buy a bigger house. Oh, and be happy. You're living the dream, after all.

* * *

My parents and I moved to Denmark in the February of 1999 because of a church ministry and teaching opportunity my dad had received. Having finished my final year of secondary school at the end of 1998 and been accepted into university, I was able to defer my tertiary studies for twelve months and move to Europe with them. The little girl marching up and down the hallway was thrilled. After one precious and memorable year, I returned to Melbourne in January 2000 to start my university degree and moved in with my sister and brother-in-law. My parents remained in Denmark, then moved to Sweden a few years later.

Those twelve months in Scandinavia as a seventeen-year-old left such an impression on my heart. The Danish people and their ways of thinking and being had got under my skin in the best possible way, and, towards the end of that year, I started dreaming in Danish. During that time, I attended a local church in Copenhagen – Kirken i Kulturcenteret (now called ARK CPH) – and played the violin in the worship team. Again, the little girl with a desire to play her instrument on European stages was thrilled. I travelled several hours each way from where we lived – in a town called Korsør – to get there on a Sunday morning for rehearsal and the service. It seemed the weekly train journey was preparing me for something, which I would come to recognise in 2012 and 2013. It was also the first time in my life I'd experienced a full cycle of the four seasons – white turning to light green, light green turning to gold, dark green turning to orange, orange turning back to white.

* * *

'Celina, I've got the feeling that we're moving out of this place next year,' Andrew said. I raised an eyebrow, unsure as to where this conversation was going. Sleep deprived, exhausted, overwhelmed, in over our heads. We were a couple of months into being new parents of our beautiful baby girl. Moving house was definitely not at the forefront of my mind. Besides, we hadn't yet reached our target for our house deposit. In our early thirties, renting a townhouse in Sydney's western suburbs, we were keen to get into the market and buy our first home. That's what everyone our age was doing, anyway. It seemed to make sense.

But when my husband gets something in his mind and heart, there's no stopping him. I watched him – partly in amusement, partly in trepidation – as he started acting on his 'feeling'. November 2011 – the lead-up to our first Christmas as a family of three – included Andrew clearing out the garage, selling things, working out what we would take with us when the day came to leave our rental for . . . well, Andrew didn't have an answer for that yet. Wonderful. The thing is, faith is contagious. It wasn't long until a yearning to move began to stir within me, too. But I did what I'm still prone to do – I tried to interpret and add to the God whispers, to make it make sense. I was adamant we would be moving into our first home in 2012. Surely that's what God was preparing us for. Surely that's what our savings were for.

* * *

I kept my head down, trying to look busy with my five-month-old, so nobody else in the parents room at my church would see my tears. It was a beautiful room – lots of light, comfortable armchairs, a kitchenette, changing tables, and boxes of nappies, wipes and toys. And a large TV screen linked to the main auditorium so you could see and hear the Sunday church service. It was Vision Sunday – an annual day held in February when our senior pastor and church leadership team share the plans for the year ahead. There was always a buzz in the air on that day. I just didn't expect the vision to include a video announcement of a particular church location starting up later that year. Now the announcement of the new church location wasn't the surprise – Hillsong Church has campuses all around the globe – I just wasn't expecting the video to feature a spinning globe, a drum roll getting louder and faster until the globe stopped spinning, and it landing on the city of the Little Mermaid and Tivoli, the red flag with the white cross. I knew it all too well. Copenhagen, Denmark.

The service concluded and I pushed the pram into the busy church foyer. I spotted Andrew. He stared at me. I stared right back at him. His eyes were still red. He had been crying, too. He now understood why he had cleared out our garage. We weren't buying our first home in Sydney. God had other plans for that money. God was calling us to move to Denmark. To help build His House – a church beckoning 'Welcome Home'.

* * *

When we arrived at Sydney International Airport on 15 September 2012, we were down to six large suitcases, several carry-on bags, two violin cases, a travel stroller and our house deposit in our bank account. Nineteen boxes holding toys, books and artwork were on a cargo ship, making their way to Copenhagen. We had sold everything else. We had reached significant peaks in our careers and then found ourselves resigning from jobs we had worked so hard towards getting – Andrew, an Undergraduate Assessment Officer for the Universities Admissions Centre and I, a Senior Education Officer for the state's Department of Education and Training – to move to the other side of the world, as volunteers, to help start a church. Some thought we were crazy. Others thought we were brave. Some thought we'd return within a year. Others were already making plans to come and visit us the year after.

Andrew and I decided to not say anything to anyone for a couple of weeks. We took time to pray and fast, needing confirmation about what we felt God had put in our hearts that day. By the April of 2012, a series of events had taken place. Firstly, Thomas, along with his wife, Katherine, who were to be the lead pastors of the church in Copenhagen, called Andrew, asking to meet up for coffee. We were in different friendship circles and had never spent time with them, so this invitation was completely out of the blue. Our names had apparently kept coming up since Vision Sunday, and Thomas had felt compelled to find out who we were. He was astonished to learn that we were prepared to move and join them in the September of that year. Next, two insightful friends reached out to us on separate occasions, both asking us flat out if we were planning to move to Denmark. One said he wanted to pay for our flights. Generosity fosters generosity. When you make plans to bless others, others get on board. Finally, my parents, who had been trying in vain for over twelve months to sell their house in Sweden to move back to Australia with my sister (who was, at that point, living in a care facility in Denmark), were growing more and more discouraged. But when we finally went public with our decision, and told them the news, their house sold that same week. And instead of moving back to Australia, they bought a place (a townhouse incidentally) in a Danish seaside village, just over an hour's drive from Copenhagen. They moved into it two weeks before we arrived.

When it's right, and when it's time, provision appears – like manna by day and quail by night.

A decision to make plans to bless

Lengthened daylight draws people outdoors in the evenings once again. This increase in sunlight generates motivation, energy and activity. Have you ever noticed how people tend to be friendlier towards strangers on a day filled with sunshine? Golden light certainly takes the edge off frustrations and delays, especially when you pause for a moment, close your eyes and turn your face to the sun. And bask. People are more than happy to extend a helpful hand and go out of their way to assist someone in need after a dose of sunshine, right?

In the same way, spring seasons in your inner world can be seasons when you have the awareness and capacity to intentionally plan acts of kindness and generosity. To notice the solo parent at your child's school who would appreciate you doing pick-up one afternoon. Organising a care package for your neighbour, who is starting cancer treatment. Taking a few extra moments to make eye contact and genuinely smile at the stressed person serving you at the grocery shop. Creating a new line in your budget to sponsor a child in a developing country or saving up to donate to a humanitarian organisation. Dropping off a homecooked meal to a frazzled couple who have just become parents and feel out of their depth. The opportunities are truly endless.

When spring enters your inner world, asking you to make plans to bless, be encouraged to do this, dear reader:

Intentionally make a difference.

Invest energy into planning how you can be generous towards others. The following verse from the book of Isaiah reveals that generosity can be more than a one-off action: it can be a permanent way of being.

> But generous people plan to do what is generous, and they stand firm in their generosity.
>
> Isaiah 32:8 NLT

Generosity isn't a personality type. It's a lifestyle anyone can choose to have. And it has nothing to do with how much money you have. People with little can be generous while people with a lot can be stingy. It's a condition of the heart and a state of the mind that characterises those who are committed to walking out their calling with purpose. It's a decision to shower others with much-needed springtime, knowing it's only a matter of time before they'll be in the position to do likewise.

CHAPTER 11:

Love – The Day My Soul Stopped Searching

October 2008, Sydney, Spring

The drive from the Hills District to the Sutherland Shire was taking forever, even on a Sunday. Sydney traffic is painful, on the best of days. My fists were clenched, and I could hear my heartbeat pulsing in my inner ear. Claire tried to distract me, chatting about light-hearted topics, over the radio. The sun shone brightly as we drove past blurs of colour – flowers in gardens happily making an appearance. We were on our way to meet Andrew. 'We' because there was no way I was going by myself. I'd only had brief interactions with him online (thank you, Facebook) and one unforgettable phone call (I really had thought my landline phone number was private – it wasn't). He seemed nice enough – super friendly, funny, interesting, articulate and undeniably good-looking – but I wasn't taking any risks; I'd called in reinforcements. The plan was for us to attend a service at Andrew's church. Afterwards, we would have coffee at a nearby café, and then . . . well, I didn't know at that point. These types of things can go either way, really.

'You need to calm down.' Claire was amused. 'What's the worst that can happen? We have a coffee with some guy, and if it doesn't go well, we just leave and drive home. You never need to see him again.' She knew that wasn't going to happen, though. Claire was pro-Andrew. And intuitive. She was doing a good job at suppressing her excitement while her best friend was freaking out in the passenger seat. We arrived at the church fifteen minutes before the service was due to start. In the foyer, I scanned the crowd, only having a Facebook profile photo to go by. Just as I thought he wasn't turning up, I locked eyes on a man making his way towards us, with a warm smile on his face that reached his kind eyes. The sound of my heartbeat started pulsing in my inner ear again when he finally arrived and stood in front of me.

* * *

After two years of working as a music and an English teacher at a secondary school in Melbourne's south-eastern suburbs, I moved to Sydney. Why? I wasn't entirely sure. I'd completed my master's degree coursework in 2005 and was in the process of writing the proposal for my thesis. Many years earlier, I'd attended a Christian conference hosted by Hillsong Church in Sydney. It was vastly different from the intimate church of thirty I attended in Melbourne, where I helped with everything from cleaning toilets, to squirting juice into tiny plastic communion cups, to setting up chairs, to singing into a microphone on my own, backing tracks accompanying our congregation's worship. No other teenagers came along, so I went to a youth group at another church.

Have you ever experienced a moment that's so brief yet profound? A moment you just know will alter the course of your life as you know it. I had one of those moments at the conference. Surrounded by thousands and thousands of people, I suddenly felt I was home. Home in Sydney. And home in that church. *Celina, one day, this will be home.* I didn't even like 'mega-churches' at the time. I didn't even like Sydney. I was a Melbournian, after all.[15]

That sense of home was quickly forgotten as the months and years flew by. Until the beginning of 2005. *Celina, one more year in Melbourne, and then it's time to move to Sydney.* It made no sense to me whatsoever, and it definitely made no sense to members of my family, my friends and my boss, who had been planning to offer me a promotion at the school. I couldn't shake the divine directive. I just knew I had to obey that small inner voice. As I made steps to move, the ground rose up to meet me. An unexpected, significant financial gift from an elderly woman in my church, which would not only cover the costs of the move but keep me going without work for around four months. The successful applicant out of dozens – without even attending the viewing – for a rental property in Sydney, a ten-minute drive from the church that was about to become my local. My application to have my Victorian teaching qualifications recognised and approved in New South Wales fast-tracked for no logical reason. My best friend's husband getting a new job, meaning that they, too, would be moving to Sydney a few months after me. Even my cynical colleague started to get in on the faith adventure. 'Any more miracles to report?' was her first question when I walked into the staffroom each morning during those months leading up to the move. The news of my resignation had spread like wildfire. As had the news of my Christian faith.

My plane landed in the city of the iconic Sydney Opera House in the January of 2006. I'd flown from Melbourne to Scandinavia to spend a month visiting and celebrating Christmas with my parents. Instead of returning to my sister and brother-in-law's place, I got in a taxi at ten o'clock at night, bound for my new rental house in a city I'd never lived in. No job, no friends, no clue. Just boxes, suitcases and a blessing in my bank account. And a church to start going to on the weekend. I was by myself, but I wasn't alone, somehow sensing this season was preparing me for something. It was a time of many beginnings: going to a new church, living in a new suburb, working as a substitute teacher for the first time, learning to navigate Sydney traffic, trying to find decent coffee.

'Hello, is this Celina Fitt?' A professional and pleasant voice. An unknown number. It was the Head of English at a school a twenty-minute drive from home. I'd been there that very morning, dropping off my CV in the hope of adding the school to my growing list of substitute teaching options. Several months had gone by, and I hadn't secured either a temporary or a permanent contract. I was thankful for the six o'clock phone calls most mornings requesting me to come in to cover for a sick teacher. 'One of my English teachers is unfortunately going through a bit of a crisis,' she went on to explain. 'She's taken an indefinite leave of absence – effective immediately – and your CV landed on my desk thirty minutes ago. Can you come in for an interview tomorrow?' I signed a contract the same day as that interview, and that temporary position eventually turned into a permanent appointment – a full-time English teacher at a multicultural high school in Sydney's western suburbs. The school that would become my case study for my master's thesis on researching pedagogical approaches to catering to cultural diversity in the classroom.

* * *

My sister, Kathy, battled with several rounds of cancer during the second half of her life on earth. Unsure of what the future held and how many years she had left, Kathy wanted to be close to our parents. She found courage to tick something off her bucket list – to travel and live in Europe. Her then-husband was up for an adventure. Together, they moved to Denmark in 2007. I was now the only person in my family living in Australia. I was about to discover and experience the power of hospitality, fellowship and community in a way that would forever define me.

* * *

'What type of guy would you like to marry one day?' the youth leader asked. I raised an eyebrow. I wasn't getting married. What guy would want to marry me? What boy would even want to ask me out on a date? A few girls giggled nervously as the youth leader encouraged us to write down a list of characteristics for our future husband. She meant well. But this was ridiculous. I was a teenager. What on earth? I didn't write anything down. The youth leader did a pretty good job of masking her disappointment when she saw my blank page. I certainly wasn't the typical pastor's kid, that's for sure. Or, maybe I was.

The stupid exercise didn't leave my mind for a few weeks. Annoyed, I surrendered, and, one afternoon after school, picked up a notebook and pen. It had been another hard day surviving the relentless bullying. Dot points. Short, at first. To my surprise, phrases and sentences soon flowed. Two pages later, I stopped writing. *As if this type of person even exists. And even if he did, as if he would be interested in me.* I closed the notebook. Well, at least I'd accomplished the task. The youth leader would be delighted, right?

* * *

Andrew and I became 'friends' online during 2007 when Facebook made its grand entrance into the World Wide Web, shoving Myspace aside – you added anyone back in those days (harsh, but undeniably true). Claire, my best friend since the age of five, was our 'mutual friend'. She had recently started studying at the same institution where Andrew worked in the student administration. Back then, 'distance education' meant someone posting you the exams (like, literally folding the papers, putting them into an addressed envelope, licking a stamp, sticking the stamp on the envelope, walking to a letter box and posting it. I know . . .). Claire nominated me to be her exam invigilator – the one fortunate enough to receive the envelopes, sit in on the exam and sign off that the student hadn't cheated (she never did). Turns out that, for almost a year, it had been Andrew writing my address on the exam envelopes and posting them. I, in turn, was the one sending them back to him. Unintentional pen pals. I recognised his handwriting long before I first shook his hand.

There was one particular incident when Claire needed help from the student administration. She got Andrew on the phone. We were out shopping, and I could overhear parts of her conversation. From what I could make out, the man on the other end must have been funny, approachable and reasonable and clearly knew what he was doing. 'Wow, that Andrew guy was really helpful! It's all sorted.' She looked at me with a grin. She was happily married. That grin was a message to me. There was only one complication – I was already in a relationship.

* * *

A violin string needs to be bound to the instrument otherwise it's of no use. But it will eventually snap suddenly if it's wound too tightly. It's a bit of a shock to the violinist when it happens. The delicate balance of binding and winding determines everything. I'd been back home from Rwanda for a couple of months. My sister had woken up from her coma after my emergency trip to Denmark. I'd used up all available leave, year twelve English exams were around the corner, and my students needed me. 'Permanent global brain damage. Permanent blindness to both eyes.' A suspected medication overdose. I will never fully know why. I'm at peace about that now – some stories are not for this side of eternity. But one thing I knew for certain – my hero was no longer by my side. I sobbed for days. And the relationship I was in was falling apart. We wanted different things, and neither of us had the courage to part ways. So, we just watched it unravel as if it was happening around us, not to us. My finances were in a mess: the events of the past months having drained my funds. And 'that Andrew guy' kept appearing on my Facebook feed.

I was wound too tightly. I snapped. Eventually suddenly. Unexpectedly expected. I was alone in the dining room and dropped to my knees onto the cold, white tiles. *You're blessed when you're at the end of your rope.*[16] It was like someone had shone a bright light into my very core, and I was horrified by what I saw. Broken pieces all over the floor. Then, hands at work. Picking up each piece, tenderly and curiously examining them. Slowly putting them together again. The pieces were me, broken by the words of a broken world. The hands belonged to my Creator. The only One who knows the original design. A burden lifted from my soul that afternoon. I didn't have to keep living the way I was. I wasn't sure what would happen next, but someone else was now in control. And the relief reduced me to tears. *With less of you there is more of God and his rule.*[17]

It was a surrender moment. You have them throughout your walk with the Lord. Mini-deaths. That bring new life. The catalyst that creates the momentum to propel you into the next season, which has been waiting for you all along. You were just stuck, needing a helpful push, which didn't feel like help in the moment. Within weeks, I ended both my relationship and my rental lease and moved into Claire and her husband's spare room to get my finances in order. Simplifying is painful to begin with, but it's more bearable than the pain of a cluttered life.

* * *

'Hello, I'm Andrew.' He leaned forward, going in for a hug. It wasn't like we were total strangers. But it was our first face-to-face meeting. I clutched my bag tightly and held out my hand instead. Handshake before hugs. Confused and amused, he took a small step back and shook it, holding my gaze. It wasn't love at first sight. Perhaps I'm too practical for that. But a frantic striving ceased within me. Peace. Coffee turned into lunch. Lunch turned into another date that same week. By the end of the month, we were officially a couple. My two-page list did exist. And it turns out he'd written a list when he was a teenager, too. My soul stopped searching. I knew home could be anywhere with Andrew next to me and with God by our side.

A decision to allow space to simplify

The weather finally gets warmer during spring. It's typically the time when people do a 'spring clean'. Houses and apartments are cleaned and rearranged, boxes are brought out from storage to pack away winter clothing, unwanted furniture items are placed on the side of the road for collection. Hedges are trimmed and tree branches are cut back. Indeed, the season of spring is a time when we want to freshen up our homes and ensure healthy growth for our gardens.

In the same way, spring seasons in your inner world can be seasons when you take stock of how you are spending your time, energy and resources. You may discover a need to declutter your thoughts and feelings, especially after a long and relentless winter.

When spring enters your inner world, asking you to allow space to simplify, be encouraged to do this, dear reader:

Honestly examine your inner world.

Life gets complicated and exhausting when we don't deal with our issues. David is courageous in Psalm 139. He boldly asks God – who is all-knowing – to point out his sin and anything in his inner world that is detrimental.

> Search me, God, and know my heart;
>   test me and know my anxious thoughts.
> See if there is any offensive way in me,
>   and lead me in the way everlasting.
>
> Psalm 139:23–24

When the Lord answers such a prayer, you can then repent, be forgiven and change your ways. Simplifying requires letting go to receive freedom and to experience wholeness and healing. To experience loving kindness in a way you never could when your soul was unnecessarily cluttered.

CHAPTER 12:

Motherhood – The Words of a Wise Woman

April 2019, Lübeck, Spring

An hour in the car, followed by a ferry ride, then a couple more hours in the car to the house that had become a place of refuge and rest since meeting the owners through mutual friends three years earlier in 2016. With more energy and vitality than people half their age, this hospitable German couple – Wolfgang and Amrie – are the epitome of generosity, wisdom and faith-filled living. With six adult children of their own, a growing number of grandchildren, and a rhythm of solitude, fellowship, creative pursuits and service, they are an encouraging example of what retirement can look and feel like. And a week with them in their family home over the Easter spring break was exactly what Andrew and I were needing. Our children, too.

* * *

We were exhausted – physically, emotionally and mentally – and going through a challenging parenting season. Not because our children were challenging, but because we really had no idea what we were doing. Raising an eight-year-old daughter and a four-year-old son with contrasting personalities, still sleep deprived, juggling jobs and serving in our church, and not having much time for ourselves was taking its toll. The hardest part was the unspoken doubt I had about my ability as a mother. All the mothers around me made parenting look so easy and flawless. Meanwhile, I was trying to read too many parenting books with no time to actually put any of the theories and tips into practice.

I also felt the intangible and unexplainable pressure for my children to behave in a certain way so that it reflected well on Andrew and me as parents, especially because we were leaders within our church. Whether you call it people pleasing, fear of what others think, striving for approval or attempting to meet unrealistic expectations, all these phrases describe the unfair cycle from which nobody comes out a winner.

* * *

There are a handful of conversations I will never forget. Timely, defining words that bring revelation, hope and relief. But first, they deliver hard truths that are difficult to hear, even though they're exactly what's needed. One of those conversations took place one morning overlooking the lake at the end of their back garden. Annika and Frederik were hunting for the Easter eggs and chocolate bunnies I had hidden earlier. It wasn't long until tears of tiredness, frustration, guilt, regret and defeat streamed down my cheeks. Amrie paused, allowing healing silence to speak more than words. Finally, a wealth of wisdom from a lifetime of experience.

'You cannot control your children; you can only control yourself. You cannot worry about what other people think of how you parent your children. Follow your intuition, trust Jesus with your children, and do what works best for your family. Raise your children individually; what you do for one may not be what you must do for the other. Praise your children more than you correct them. Choose connection over compliance. And remember: you're doing better than you think you are.'

I exhaled, and realised I had been holding my breath. For the first time in a long time, I felt a burden lifted and, in its place, the soothing balm of hope.

A decision to look ahead with expectation

Spring presents us with signs of new life, which bring great joy and delight. The sound of birds singing early in the morning, flower seedlings sprouting through the soil, new leaves appearing on trees and animals being born remind us that positive change is in the air.

In the same way, spring seasons in your inner world can be seasons when both unexpected and long-awaited changes start to take place. The intangible fog of slumber finally lifts. Winter's past seems distant, and summer's promise seems close.

When spring enters your inner world, asking you to look ahead with expectation, be encouraged to do this, dear reader:

Confidently place your hope in Jesus.

It's easy to lose your hope during winter, but when spring enters your soul, it brings fresh hope and energy that enables you to expect and embrace change. King Solomon penned Song of Songs, telling of the love between a bride and groom, to affirm the sanctity of marriage and to illustrate God's love for His people.

> The season has changed, the bondage of your barren winter has ended, and the season of hiding is over and gone. The rains have soaked the earth and left it bright with blossoming flowers. The season for singing and pruning the vines has arrived. I hear the cooing of doves in our land, filling the air with songs to awaken you and guide you forth. Can you not discern this new day of destiny breaking forth around you? The early signs of my purposes and plans are bursting forth. The budding vines of new life are now blooming everywhere. The fragrance of their flowers whispers, "There is change in the air."
>
> Song of Songs 2:11–13a TPT

Good things are coming your way! It's time for a revival of hope. And we can place our unfailing hope in Jesus who *is* hope – 'an anchor for the soul, firm and secure' (Hebrews 6:19).

PART III –

Cadence

A decision to take steps of faith: bravely act on your dreams.
A decision to make plans to bless: intentionally make a difference.
A decision to allow space to simplify: honestly examine your inner world.
A decision to look ahead with expectation: confidently place your hope in Jesus.

PART IV —

Summer's Harvest

Allegro non molto
Under a hard Season, fired up by the Sun
Languishes man, languishes the flock and burns the pine.
We hear the cuckoo's voice;
then sweet songs of the turtledove and finch are heard.
Soft breezes stir the air, but threatening
the North Wind sweeps them suddenly aside.
The shepherd trembles,
fearing violent storms and his fate.

Adagio e piano – presto e forte
The fear of lightning and fierce thunder
Robs his tired limbs of rest
As gnats and flies buzz furiously around.

Presto
Alas, his fears were justified.
The Heavens thunder and roar and with hail
Cut the head off the wheat and damage the grain.[18]

PRELUDE –

Action

For agricultural workers, summer is a season of productivity and abundance – a season of glorious fruitfulness! Jesus expects His followers to be fruitful. In fact, when you turn to the very beginning of the Bible – the book of Genesis in the Old Testament – the very first blessing and mandate that God spoke over humanity was in regard to fruitfulness:

> So God created mankind in his own image, in the image of God he created them; male and female he created them. God blessed them and said to them, "Be fruitful and increase in number; fill the earth and subdue it..."
>
> Genesis 1:27–28a

In the New Testament, Jesus reaffirms this mandate.

> "You did not choose me, but I chose you and appointed you so that you might go and bear fruit—fruit that will last—and so that whatever you ask in my name the Father will give you."
>
> John 15:16

Notice that Jesus doesn't just talk about 'fruit'; He specifically refers to 'fruit that will last'. He talks about living flourishing lives that make an eternal impact. Fruit that lasts is about who we are becoming – our character. It's about growing in the fruit of the spirit: love, joy, peace, patience, kindness, goodness, faithfulness and self-control.[19] Fruit that lasts means fulfilling God's purpose and plan for your life, and following His will, not living for yourself.

Here are four actions that summer requires of you, which I believe will help you recognise and understand summer when it arrives in your inner world:

1. An action to bring in your abundance
2. An action to stand firm in your field
3. An action to kneel on your threshing floor
4. An action to lift your eyes to new horizons

Remember, this sacred season is about gathering in the harvest.

All will be well. Just take action.

CHAPTER 13:

Grief and Healing – Create with Words

July 2022, Venice, Summer

Thank you for emailing me at Create with Celina Mina. I am currently away on summer holiday and will be back to work on Monday 1 August 2022. I will reply to your email when I return. Kind regards, Celina.

Out of Office set. The final thing left on my list. I closed my laptop and exhaled. Andrew was loading the never-ending row of bags that had snaked their way from the lounge down the hallway, and to the front door of our apartment. Annika and Frederik were giddy with excitement. Time for our family road trip adventure to Italy, which we'd been planning for several months. *Times of refreshing are coming from the Lord.*[20] I needed it.

* * *

A learning curve. A process where people develop a skill by learning from their mistakes. A steep learning curve. The same thing, but doing it very quickly. Dictionary definitions are helpful, but they don't quite prepare you for being so steep that you're about to fall off the curve. Essentially, a roller coaster, which may or may not be attached to the track depending on the day.

I'd left a profession where every minute of your working day is determined for you – where you need to be, what you need to teach, who you're teaching it to. I was no longer an employee – focused on the core work, not wondering if there would be a pay slip at the end of each month. I never thought I'd be full-time in my own business – CEO, COO, CFO, HR, every other acronym rolled into one. Invoices, contracts, GDPR, marketing strategies, social media scheduling, equipment purchases, tax law, workflows, admin, meetings, algorithms, reports from the accountant, working across time zones, diplomatically informing an author that it will take longer than a month for their draft to become a published book on a shelf. Oh, and the billable stuff that equates to food on the table. Those first couple of years were exhilarating, terrifying, frustrating, rewarding and wonderfully fulfilling. I never regretted resigning from my full-time teaching position and allowing my mental health crisis to be the catalyst – it propelled me onto a new career path.

***

The money still wasn't in my account. The invoice had been sent. The due date had come and gone. Automated reminder notices. Unanswered emails. The dawning realisation that the client wasn't paying me. Christmas of 2020 was a couple of weeks away. It was getting harder to suppress the panic and desperation bubbling beneath the surface. We actually need these moments of sheer desperation. Sorry to be the bearer of bad (good) news. It reveals who or what we are truly placing our trust in. And this set of circumstances revealed that I was placing my trust in a client. An invoice. How quickly we forget.

'Celina, you are not self-employed. I am your employer. And I'm a good boss. Bring your desperation to me and to me alone.'

Then, five more words. 'Have I ever not provided?'

Tears of repentance. The only response to such a question. I was trusting in my own strength. We do that when desperation hits. Fight-flight-freeze-or-fawn kicks in, and we need to learn to choose faith instead. I'd done the work; I'd done all I could. It was time to stop and wait upon the Lord. *The name of the Lord is a strong tower; the righteous run to it and are safe. Jehovah Jireh. My provider. Jehovah Rapha. My healer. Jehovah Shalom. My peace.* It all came back to me. Every season is preparation for the next.

A notification popped up on the screen. The payment had been made. Tears again. This time of gratitude and relief. It was a needed lesson and a reminder for the years ahead. My good boss always provides. He never fails.

* * *

'Our next stop is Burano. Remember to take all your bags and belongings with you; do not leave anything on the boat. We depart in two hours for the next island. We wish you an enjoyable time exploring Burano.'

Have you ever made a spontaneous decision that proved to be a brilliant decision? This was one of them. Upon our arrival in Caorle, a coastal town of the Metropolitan City of Venice, the helpful woman on reception at our accommodation handed us a stack of brochures in English. As I thumbed through one of them, a glossy advertisement caught my eye. A one-day boat cruise of the islands of Murano, Burano and Torcello in the Venetian Lagoon. 'Let's do this!' I exclaimed.

Nothing quite prepares your soul for an encounter with sheer beauty. Church bells welcomed us as we stepped off the boat and made our way into Burano's centre. We turned a corner, and I stopped dead in my tracks. 'Mummy, what's wrong? Are you okay?' Frederik was concerned. I didn't realise that I'd gasped loudly and put my hand to my chest. Rows of buildings standing like soldiers side by side, each one a vibrant colour. Canary. Lime. Tangerine. Magenta. Crimson. Lilac. Indigo. Violet. Cobalt. Emerald. Fuchsia. All against the backdrop of a cerulean sky. Leafy vines laden with flowers in full bloom formed living patterns. Legend has it that the buildings were painted such bright colours to prevent the fishermen from crashing their boats into the island in the fog.

Words do the same thing. They also stand like soldiers side by side, each one evoking an emotion, colouring the imagination, telling a story to serve as a life jacket, preventing people from capsizing and drowning. 'Hey, let's keep going.' Andrew put his arm around me. 'We only have a couple of hours here.' Yes, time is short. So, we need to keep going. We need to tell our stories. We need to create with words and paint rainbows of promise in the stormy sky so those who see them keep going, too.

An action to bring in your abundance

Summer creates a tension. Within an industrialised society and for city-dwellers, summer is synonymous with holiday time. However, for farmers, it's peak season. I dare you to tell a farmer to go and take a holiday during summer! For them, it's a season of undivided focus – blood, sweat and tears. Nothing else matters because it's time for harvest and reaping the crops. Fruit, vegetables and grain are ripe, and the sounds of harvesting machines and equipment can be heard across farmlands.

Now I'm not suggesting we shouldn't take holidays during summer. However, when summer seasons enter your inner world, it might be time to roll up your sleeves and get to work. The grief and healing process can feel never-ending and span months, years, decades – a lifetime. However, great and lasting fruitfulness can still come out of soul-crushing limitation, debilitating pain and life-altering diagnosis. There can still be opportunities for personal success, meaningful work and fulfilling accomplishment.

When summer enters your inner world, asking you to bring in your abundance, remember this, dear reader:

Fruitfulness involves faithfulness, strategy and hard work.

The writer of Proverbs draws upon observations of and inspiration from nature to illustrate principles for living life well.

> Take a lesson from the ants, you lazybones.
>   Learn from their ways and become wise!
> Though they have no prince
>   or governor or ruler to make them work,
> they labor hard all summer,
>   gathering food for the winter.
> But you, lazybones, how long will you sleep?
>   When will you wake up?
> A little extra sleep, a little more slumber,
>   a little folding of the hands to rest—
> then poverty will pounce on you like a bandit;
>   scarcity will attack you like an armed robber.

Proverbs 6:6–11 NLT

Gathering in the harvest doesn't just happen by itself. God can put a dream in your heart. God can give you a glimpse into what the future holds. However, a time comes when God says, 'Go for it! Grab a hold of that opportunity! Pursue that connection! Invest your energy, time and finances into that project! Work for it! It's yours!' So, to the best of our ability, knowing that His strength is made perfect in our weakness, we embrace abundance. We allow recovery to lead us to the golden fields.

CHAPTER 14:

Calling – The Decade of Miraculous Provision

August 2022, Copenhagen, Summer

'If you could choose one word to describe your first decade living in Denmark, what would it be?' The question caught me by surprise. But I shouldn't have been surprised. Andrew and I were having lunch with a man who had become a dear mentor and friend to us over the years. He was visiting Copenhagen one month before we were due to celebrate ten years of living in Denmark. Time with Robert always refreshed the soul and involved many questions just like this one. 'Just one word?' Andrew and I looked at each other, eyes wide, thinking. 'Well,' I began, 'this past decade has revealed to us, more than ever before, how God is *Jehovah Jireh*. So, I guess the word would be . . . *provision*.' I choked on the last word as tears filled my eyes.

* * *

It took us just over twenty-four hours to get from Australia to Denmark in September 2012. But it took us nine months to move from my parents' home into our first apartment in Copenhagen in June 2013. Humbling, to say the least. Humility (with, perhaps, a dose of humiliation) is often the result of coming up with your own plan of how things should be, only to come to the stark realisation that the universe didn't get the memo: *Plan? What plan? You have a plan? All the best with that.*

Our first nine months were difficult and exhausting. Even though it was a blessing to have accommodation, it was a six-hour return trip to

Copenhagen using public transport. Seven hours on a Sunday. Walk. Bus. Intercity train. City train. Walk. Sometimes, another bus. Walk. And we did this four times per week, our one-year-old in tow, attending church social gatherings, planning meetings and services. Winter was long; the snow lasted from late November 2012 to early April 2013. Our savings were steadily decreasing, and Andrew had applied for nearly seventy jobs. Because that was our plan: I would stay at home with Annika for a little while longer, Andrew would be the first one to get a job, and then we would get our own apartment in Copenhagen. All within a couple of months, of course. *How are you going with your plan, Celina?* Great, just great.

'Could you start doing some substitute teaching?' Belinda asked curiously. 'In the international schools in Copenhagen?' We were so thankful for our friends from Australia, who invested their time and finances to visit us, especially during those early days. We were showing Belinda, her husband and son around the city we ourselves hadn't yet moved to. We were three months into living in Denmark. It's obvious to me now, but at that point, Belinda's question was a brightly lit light bulb that cleared out the darkness. When you're fixated on your own plan, you become narrow-minded and need someone to flick the switch for you. I could feel Andrew staring at me. He had also heard the gentle, wise suggestion clothed as a question. From that moment, the plan changed. Or rather, I laid down my own plan and saw what God had been patiently waiting for me to see and how He had already prepared us for it – Andrew remaining home with Annika while I found work as a teacher in the English-speaking schools. After all, didn't I have a master's in education, specialising in . . . that's right, international education?

***

By the April of 2013, several international schools had approved me to be an on-call substitute teacher, and I was getting at least one, usually two to three, days per week of work. To get to Copenhagen from Skælskør by the start of the school day meant waking up at four o'clock. If there was a church meeting that evening, plus work the next day, hospitable families from our growing church community would let me stay the night. There were weeks when I barely saw Andrew and Annika, and, no sooner would my wages go into our account, it would go out again, bringing the balance back down to almost zero – our 'first home in Sydney deposit' had served its God-intended purpose. We were now living 'daily-bread days'. Do you know what happens when our Triune God holds bread in His hands? He breaks it. Then, it multiplies.

At least the snow was clearing, and the days were getting longer – brighter, warmer. The birds knew it, too. They had returned home, chirping their greetings. Winter had turned to spring. The warmer days meant my parents could now begin renovating their townhouse. This meant we needed to be out by June. The intangible button on the unspoken countdown clock had been pressed. We had just over a month to move out and get our own place in Copenhagen. And we had two hundred kroner (around forty Aussie dollars) to make that happen. Impossible, right? Well, impossible is exactly where Jehovah Jireh loves to make His appearance. We just didn't know that then like we do now.

* * *

Andrew responded to our desperate situation the way he knew how – he started packing boxes and suitcases. He was becoming remarkably good at it. After all, things seemed to happen when he packed. We also got down on our knees. Literally. And prayed. More like cried. Words in between muffled sobs. I don't really know what I was expecting to happen next. We often want God's response to our pleas to come in the form of the heavens parting and a choir of angels singing in perfect harmony. Well, that didn't happen. What *did* happen a few days later was a text message. *Hi Celina, I went running with a friend over the weekend. Turns out she knows you, too – you're subbing at both our schools. We talked about how you live so far away. Do you need to rent an apartment in Copenhagen? Mine is available. Would you like to see it before I advertise it? It's available as of next month.* Next month. That would be June. 'Let's go and see it,' Andrew said. 'But we don't have any money!' I replied – glass half empty. 'I think that's the point,' said Andrew – glass half full.

I had been studying the book of Esther, using a Bible study by Beth Moore. Her teaching videos and accompanying workbook nourished my soul during those desperate months. I concluded the final session the week we were to view the apartment. The study exhorted me to remember and follow the ways of Esther – her wisdom, her teachable heart, her faith, her courage – and to expect deliverance. After all, God turns the tables and reverses destinies when He intervenes. 'Do you have the address?' asked Andrew. Good point. We only had the suburb name – and I already knew it was one of the most expensive parts of Copenhagen. The irony was not lost on us, knowing our bank balance. I sent the owner a message to clarify. She quickly replied with the details. Oh, and this extra bit of helpful information: *The street can be a bit tricky to work out. When you come out of the train station, just follow* Esthersvej *all the way down. The street connects to that.* I blinked in disbelief. Just follow *Esthersvej*. Literal translation? *The way of Esther*. Deliverance had appeared – in the form of an apartment in Copenhagen.

It was like Christmas Day that first week of June 2013, when we opened those nineteen boxes that had been sitting in a storage warehouse near my parents' place since November 2012. Annika squealed in pure delight as she caught sight of her first birthday presents – toys that had been played with briefly at her party but packed away that same day. Andrew hung up paintings on the walls with a grin on his face. I wiped silent tears as I placed book after book after book on the shelves – each one a long-lost friend who had finally made it home. The apartment was everything we had hoped for, and more. Large windows and high ceilings ushered in light; wooden floorboards lengthened the rooms; a little private garden surrounded by a hedge kept Annika entertained and safe; a bathroom that didn't have the shower directly over the toilet (if you know, you know). As for the 'more' – a wonderful community of neighbours, who have remained friends over the years, even after we moved five years later. And the apartment was fully furnished, which would turn out to be a blessing during those first five years while we slowly recovered financially from the move.

Which begs the question, *how did the finances come together so we could move in?* Within forty-eight hours of viewing the apartment, we received an email from a couple who were living in New York City at the time. They had been praying for us, without knowing the specifics of our situation, and wrote to say that if we ever needed financial help to get into a property in Copenhagen, they would help us. We just needed to reach out when the time came. 'Well, I believe that time is now!' Andrew and I burst into laughter. We hadn't laughed with such joy in quite a while. Psalm 126:5–6 was right. *Those who sow with tears will reap with songs of joy. Those who go out weeping, carrying seed to sow, will return with songs of joy, carrying sheaves with them.*

* * *

Someone once told me life is often a series of problem-solving exercises. Like a maths test. One exercise appears, and you've barely finished writing down the solution before the next one arrives on the page. That's precisely how those first two years felt – September 2012 to September 2014. But God is the ultimate mathematician. He's already at work behind us, next to us and ahead of us, putting solutions in place before the problems even surface. While the generosity of that beloved couple helped us with the deposit and the first few months of rent, we had no idea how everything else was going to work out. Something, however, had changed within us. Worry had been replaced by expectation. Fear had been replaced by excitement. 'What are we going to do now?' had changed to 'What is God going to do next?' Well, there were a lot of 'nexts' . . .

Andrew happened to stumble upon an advertisement for a part-time maternity-leave music teaching position at an international school – one I hadn't taught at. The deadline to apply was close of business that very day, leaving me with a couple of hours to hit submit. One online interview later, I got the job and started in September 2013. In that same month, someone from our church asked me to proofread their PhD thesis. I agreed and set up a sole trader company so I could invoice and receive payment in accordance with Danish tax rules. By the January of 2014, the teacher on maternity leave announced she was resigning and was moving to Asia. I applied for the permanent full-time position, which would commence that August after summer break. The requirement to apply? Postgraduate studies specialising in international education. I was the successful candidate. Tears flowed (again) as I reviewed and signed the contract.

Andrew remained home, helping Annika get settled into the final months of *vuggestue* (Danish childcare) in preparation for her starting *børnehave* (Danish kindergarten). He volunteered his time to complete administrative tasks for our church and built friendships with members of the congregation. We were living by faith (one part-time salary and some freelance work to support a family of three in Copenhagen wasn't cutting it), and this book isn't long enough to share every detail, every story, every act of God's provision. But let me share a little bit of the manna and quail with you, dear reader.

Andrew and I started hosting a fortnightly church connect group in our apartment, which included a potluck dinner. Some weeks, our fridge was more shelves than food. Our guests would leave, saying 'just keep the leftovers', and we'd watch those leftovers literally multiply as we spooned them into plastic containers. Once, when we were still living at my parents' place, we were down to one nappy and no baby wipes (every parent's nightmare). And we were getting ready to house-sit an apartment in Copenhagen. When it came time for the couple to say goodbye, before heading for the airport, the wife pointed to a bag of cans and bottles. 'So sorry for not getting round to that! We ran out of time. The next time you're at the shops, would you please return them? Just keep the money.' Andrew returned promptly from the shops – those cans and bottles were exactly enough for a bag of nappies and a packet of baby wipes (parents, sigh with relief). Unexpected bags of groceries appeared at our door. We arrived at the train station to go to church, knowing we didn't have enough money for the tickets, only to get a message from someone – just as we arrived at the machine – saying they had transferred a gift into our account. We got to church that day. I hadn't had my hair done for almost a year, and a woman who worked for L'Oréal Denmark gave me a gift bag containing shampoo, conditioner, treatments and hair colour. 'Because you're worth it,' Anne-Laure said with a wink. I laughed. Then promptly bawled my eyes out.

By the May of 2014, Andrew still hadn't got a job. Twenty months. I think a man's strength is revealed when his status symbols are stripped away. I think a man's heart is revealed when those symbols are then reinstated – no longer seen through the eyes of being 'self-made', but from a soul of humble gratitude, dependent on the One who both gives and takes away.[21]

I was at our desk, working on a sermon. I had started receiving unexpected opportunities from my pastors to preach at church. Andrew was sitting in our garden. 'Celina, now watch what I'm about to do.' Crystal clear. Still, small voice. When God moves, He moves. Quickly. The sound of his phone ringing. Totally eavesdropping, I caught fragments – 'Which job was that?' 'Starting next month?' 'Where will the interview be?' Eyes wide, hands slightly shaking, Andrew comes inside. 'That was UNICEF. I didn't get a job I applied for ages ago, but they kept my details in a talent pool for future roles.'

For twenty months, Andrew hadn't bought any new clothes except for a winter jacket and winter boots. We were amazed they hadn't faded from the constant wear. The day he got the job, they started to fall apart – buttons fell off shirts, rips appeared in jeans, sleeves of T-shirts unravelled, zips broke off jumpers. 'What on earth am I going to wear to work?' Andrew stared into his wardrobe in dismay. A few days later, at the playground with Annika, a neighbour called Jacob, who owned a men's clothing store in our area, arrived with his son. He looked at Andrew and asked him his size. Random question at a playground, right? Nothing's random. Especially when it turns out he 'just happened' to have bags of trousers, shirts and jumpers his boutique no longer needed. Especially when they 'just happened' to be in Andrew's size.

* * *

'Thank you for our time together,' Andrew said, giving Robert a hug at the end of our lunch. I was still composing myself, having cried through most of it, after telling stories of God's faithfulness over the past ten years. Stories of miraculous provision during our first decade in Denmark. Yes, provision. Not too much, not too little, not too late, not too early. Always what was needed, exactly on time. For the Israelites wandering the wilderness, Jehovah Jireh's provision appeared as manna by day and quail by night. But they were slowly walking towards a season when the next generation would enter the Promised Land, overflowing with milk and honey.[22] Provision for the day would soon turn into abundance for a lifetime.

An action to stand firm in your field

Summer is a season of extremes. You can be engulfed by intense heat for hours, then caught off guard by a sudden thunderstorm and downpour. What's remarkable about farmers is their resilience. They don't give up on the harvest when it gets too hot or when thunder and lightning strike. They remain undistracted and unmoving from the task at hand. They remain in their field because the stakes are high and they know their place and the part they play.

In the same way, summer seasons in your inner world can be seasons when you want to give up on something because it's suddenly got hard. 'Giving up' is an emotive phrase with negative connotations that can stir up feelings of defensiveness and shame. It's also helpfully and unhelpfully subjective – giving up can mean something entirely different from one person to the next, from one set of circumstances to the next.

When summer enters your inner world, asking you to stand firm in your field, remember this, dear reader:

Fruitfulness involves obstacles, challenge and adversity.

In his letter to the believers in Ephesus, the Apostle Paul endeavours to strengthen and encourage them to stand firm in their Christian faith.

> Finally, be strong in the Lord and in his mighty power. Put on the full armor of God, so that you can take your stand against the devil's schemes. For our struggle is not against flesh and blood, but against the rulers, against the authorities, against the powers of this dark world and against the spiritual forces of evil in the heavenly realms. Therefore put on the full armor of God, so that when the day of evil comes, you may be able to stand your ground, and after you have done everything, to stand.

Ephesians 6:10–13.

As followers of Jesus, we need to remember that while God has a plan for our lives, so does the enemy. Jesus's plan for your life is fruitfulness. The enemy's plan is to destroy your fruit and to stop the process of further fruitfulness. The enemy knows he can't take away your salvation, but he can try and stop you from bearing fruit. He can try and shift your gaze from your calling. A bit of discouragement here. An unexpected situation there. Distractions, disappointments, defeats. Don't get shocked when you have to face the heat or thunderstorms that come your way during summer. What do you do when these things inevitably come your way?

> Stand firm then, with the belt of truth buckled around your waist, with the breastplate of righteousness in place, and with your feet fitted with the readiness that comes from the gospel of peace. In addition to all this, take up the shield of faith, with which you can extinguish all the flaming arrows of the evil one. Take the helmet of salvation and the sword of the

> Spirit, which is the word of God.
>
> And pray in the Spirit on all occasions with all kinds of prayers and requests. With this in mind, be alert and always keep on praying for all the Lord's people.
>
> Ephesians 6:14–18

You have what you need: truth, righteousness, readiness, the gospel of peace, faith, salvation, the Word, prayer. Stand firm.

CHAPTER 15:

Love – The Sermon I Don't Remember on a Sunday I'll Never Forget

December 2007, Melbourne, Summer

Sermons, messages, talks. Whatever you call them, I've listened to countless of them – Sunday services, mid-week events, conferences, weddings, funerals. I'd like to say I remember all of them, but let's be real; unless you take notes and go over them later, you're likely to forget most of what you heard within twenty-four hours. There's one sermon I wish I'd brought along my notebook and pen to. Sunday 30 December 2007. I was twenty-six years old. After almost two years of living in Sydney, I was back in Melbourne spending Christmas with my best friend, her husband and their extended families, trying to distract myself from worrying about a complicated relationship that was waiting for me upon my return after New Year's Eve. We went along to a service at a vibrant, friendly local church. Not completely present, I was admittedly thinking about how guilty I felt about not being in Scandinavia to spend Christmas with my parents, Kathy and my then brother-in-law – finances hadn't worked out that year. The preacher then got up to speak. 'What if your life could be totally different in exactly one year's time from today?' He had my attention. Tears began forming. The Biblical passage was taken from Genesis – the story of the life of Joseph.[23] I don't remember the main points or the other analogies. Just that opening question. Oh, and kneeling during the ministry time at the end. 'I want to pray for anyone here today who desperately wants their life to be totally different this time next year. You need a dramatic turnaround. If that's you, just raise your hand, or perhaps kneel exactly where you are as I pray.' My knees touched the floor before my brain caught up with what my heart was doing. That's when you know you're surrendering.

* * *

Andrew and I met and got married within six months. Not recommended for every couple (disclaimer), but despite concerned warnings from some well-meaning friends, our six-month timeline was exactly what we both needed. Nonetheless, a short courtship and engagement meant intentionally squeezing in hours and hours of challenging conversations in the midst of enjoying the romance of it all and doing fun things such as booking honeymoon flights. *Do you want to have kids? How many? What if it turns out we can't? Do you have any debt? What did you love and hate most about your childhood? Have you ever been addicted to anything? Do you always want to live in Australia? Anything from past relationships that could affect our marriage?* I know. Sounds like an interrogation. But with a coffee while taking a long walk.

The couple facilitating our pre-marriage counselling course were wise, hilarious, authentic and generous. 'Couples can spend so much of their engagement preparing for their wedding day, without thinking much about years and years of their marriage.' Another pearl: 'You don't have to have it all together before the wedding day. In fact, some areas of brokenness are healed during the course of marriage.' Well, that was a relief to hear. And a much-needed blessing.

* * *

The day had got off to a great start. A delicious brunch at Cafe Europa in the heart of Copenhagen. I was having a blast being the tour guide, showing Andrew around my favourite European city. Taking in the panoramic views from the top of the Rundetårn. Watching ice-skaters at Kongens Nytorv. The mandatory photo of Nyhavn 17. Proving that Den Lille Havfrue is significantly smaller than tourists expect. Ending the day with a celebratory dinner and rides at Tivoli before my dad picked us up. There was one other place we visited that afternoon.

Where is he? Having been standing next to me literally seconds earlier,

Andrew had vanished. I slowly turned a full 360 degrees, carefully scanning the four identical buildings that make up Amalienborg, the official palace of the Danish royal family. He was nowhere in sight. A passer-by caught my eye and smiled knowingly. I gave a blank stare of confusion in return. 'Ahem' – the sound of someone clearing their throat, attempting to get my attention. I looked down in the direction of the sound. Andrew had been right in front of me all along. Down on one knee, a grin on his face. The date of the proposal? Monday 29 December 2008. The next day, I'd wake up an engaged woman. A dramatic turnaround within a year, starting with my kneeling in doubt and despair and ending with Andrew kneeling in anticipation and joy.

An action to kneel on your threshing floor

Here's what you need to know about threshing floors if you're not too familiar with them: in Biblical times, crops were taken to the threshing floor once they'd been gathered into sheaves. Threshing crops loosens the edible grain and the husks from the straw. The grain is beaten and trodden upon. Winnowing then separates the grain from the chaff. The grain is thrown up into the air so the wind can blow away the chaff, and the heavy grain kernels fall back down to the ground to be collected.

In the same way, summer seasons in your inner world can be when you need to let go of certain things, count the cost and pay the price. Threshing floor moments when you can choose to remain on that floor or walk away from it. There's always a choice and there's always a consequence.

When summer enters your inner world, asking you to kneel on your threshing floor, remember this, dear reader:

Fruitfulness involves sacrifice, separation and surrender.

David understood that giving to God that which costs nothing does not demonstrate commitment nor does it lead to fruitfulness. Sacrifice, separation and surrender – though difficult – must be done voluntarily and truly mean something.

> David said to him, "Let me have the site of your threshing floor so I can build an altar to the Lord, that the plague on the people may be stopped. Sell it to me at the full price." Araunah said to David, "Take it! Let my lord the king do whatever pleases him. Look, I will give the oxen for the burnt offerings, the threshing sledges for the wood, and the wheat for the grain offering. I will give all this." But King David replied to Araunah, "No, I insist on paying the full price. I will not take for the Lord what is yours, or sacrifice a burnt offering that costs me nothing." So David paid Araunah six hundred shekels of gold for the site. David built an altar to the Lord there and sacrificed burnt offerings and fellowship offerings. He called on the Lord, and the Lord answered him with fire from heaven on the altar of burnt offering.
>
> 1 Chronicles 21:22–26

> Then Solomon began to build the temple of the Lord in Jerusalem on Mount Moriah, where the Lord had appeared to his father David. It was on the threshing floor of Araunah the Jebusite, the place provided by David.
>
> 2 Chronicles 3:1

David built an altar on the threshing floor, the site upon which his son built the temple of the Lord. A legacy of sacrifice resulting in loving worship. Our threshing floor moments are never just about ourselves; they are about the generations to come. Throughout our Christian experience, you will often find yourself on the threshing floor. The Holy Spirit will lovingly, yet firmly, confront certain things in our lives and say, 'Do you want to be fruitful? Then you need to separate from that now. You need to sacrifice that now. You need to surrender that now.' Please remain on the threshing floor. It will become a temple's foundation.

CHAPTER 16:

Motherhood – Fifty, Twenty, Sixteen

July 2022, Öland, Summer

After two weeks in Venice, Italy, we headed to the blue and white wooden summer house on an island off the south-eastern coast of Sweden. It belongs to Andrew's best friend's family, and we were thrilled to spend a whole week with Carl-Hugo and his wife, Amanda, and their two children to conclude our three-week summer holiday. Amid celebrating Carl-Hugo's fortieth birthday and twenty years of the men's friendship, meaningful conversations about parenting seasons and our journeys thus far refreshed our souls.

* * *

'Where do you come from?' A simple question with a complex answer. A British father, a Filipino-Chinese-Spanish mother, born in Auckland, raised in Melbourne, a permanent resident of Denmark. The epitome of multiculturalism. Brexit – the withdrawal of the United Kingdom from the European Union – became a reality a couple of years after we applied for and received permanent residency in Denmark. Such a relief, considering how much more complicated it is for non-EU citizens to be granted PR status in Denmark. I never would have imagined having two children who culturally identify so differently. The question 'where do you come from?' results in one child responding, 'I'm Australian but raised in Denmark' and the other, 'I'm Danish with Australian parents.' After many conversations and unexpected circumstances, we realised that, unlike the 'normal' majority, our children needed different schools – two different types of education. One in the international school system and one in the local Danish school system. It was just like Amrie had said to me several years earlier: 'Celina, follow your intuition. It doesn't matter what other people think about how you and Andrew are raising your children. What works for one child won't necessarily work for the other, and that's okay.'

* * *

It was getting late. The long Scandinavian summer day was finally shifting to darkness, and we were getting ready for bed, the children already peacefully asleep. That's when the most out-of-the-blue thoughts seem to present themselves – either first thing upon waking or last thing before drifting off to sleep. The four of us had been talking about how our ten-year anniversary of living in Denmark was only a few months away – the next decade and the rest of our forties. 'When I turn fifty, Annika will be turning twenty. She'll have finished secondary school and have already started the next stage of her life, whatever that will be. Frederik will be turning sixteen and in his final year of school.' My revelation tumbled out of my mouth before my mind could thoroughly process it. I was no longer tired, and I tossed and turned for hours before finally falling asleep just as the sun was rising again.

* * *

At the time of writing this book, our next decade is probably our final decade of having both children at home with us. The days are slow and long, but the years are fast and short. And with our children rapidly growing up right before our eyes, we have had a shift in thinking and perspective when it comes to parenting. Not just raising our children, but discipling our children. Not just parenting our children, but pastoring our children. Not just fixing our eyes on the here and now, but lifting our eyes to the horizon – making the most of this sacred calling and opportunity to prepare the next generation to be more and do more than we could ever have hoped for or imagined.

Change is in the air, once again.

An action to lift your eyes to new horizons

Summer is filled with humid days and balmy nights. There is something slightly unnerving, disorienting and intriguing about hazy horizons; they are unclear and undefined, yet attractive and alluring.

In the same way, summer seasons in your inner world can be when you sense there's something new on the horizon, but you can't make out what. It feels unsettling, yet exciting. Vague, yet promising. We want certainty and clarity, yet desire adventure and risk at the same time. It's a season of being open to the Lord's fresh leading in our lives.

When summer enters your inner world, asking you to lift your eyes to new horizons, remember this, dear reader:

Fruitfulness involves fresh vision, opportunity and change.

The danger of fruitfulness is that once you start experiencing success, you can become more consumed by the fruit you have, rather than by the harvests in your future. Your fruitfulness from one summer becomes the resource that enables you to do the work for the next harvest. There is still so much more in store!

During his ministry on earth, Jesus modelled being simultaneously present and acutely aware of the future.

> When he saw the vast crowds of people, Jesus' heart was deeply moved with compassion, because they seemed weary and helpless, like wandering sheep without a shepherd. He turned to his disciples and said, "The harvest is huge and ripe! But there are not enough harvesters to bring it all in. As you go, plead with the Owner of the Harvest to thrust out many more reapers to harvest his grain!"
>
> Matthew 9:36–38 TPT

Jesus always looks at the harvest waiting in the horizon. Therefore, you need to do what this Scripture describes:

> Keep your eyes on Jesus, who both began and finished this race we're in. Study how he did it. Because he never lost sight of where he was headed—that exhilarating finish in and with God—he could put up with anything along the way: Cross, shame, whatever. And now he's there, in the place of honor, right alongside God.
>
> Hebrews 12:2 MSG

Jesus's crucifixion and resurrection embodies everything about fruitfulness. It exemplifies everything about reaping, standing firm, sacrifice, and the generations. For the Lamb of God that was slain is indeed the Lord of the Harvest. That harvest is *you*.

PART IV –

Cadence

An action to bring in your abundance: involves faithfulness, strategy and hard work.
An action to stand firm in your field: involves obstacles, challenge and adversity.
An action to kneel on your threshing floor: involves separation, sacrifice and surrender.
An action to lift your eyes to new horizons: involves fresh vision, opportunity and change.

. . . back to autumn, friend.

PART V –

Transition's Value

Overrated
Rated or valued too highly,
Possibly causing both disappointment and relief

Underrated
Not rated or valued highly enough,
Possibly creating both happiness and sorrow

Autumn, transition, winter
Transition, spring, transition
Summer, transition
Repeat . . .

PRELUDE –

Lesson

There is a fifth season. It comes around more often than you think, yet its value is usually missed. It's a season that is underrated, therefore we don't have a revelation of how important it actually is. What is this underrated season? It's the season of transition. Not to be confused with autumn's shifts and change, transition is a period when things seem to take longer than expected. It could even mean facing something not changing on this side of eternity – a health condition, a relationship status, a financial consequence – and coming to terms with moving forward in spite of that.

Transition is moving away from what was and towards what could be. One set of circumstances and one way of being and thinking, to another set of circumstances and a new way of being and thinking. Involving inner formation and transformation – a *metamorphosis*, if you will – it combines elements of both what was and what will be. A discomforting, bittersweet mix of anticipation and dread. Our default is to rush through transition as quickly as possible, to get on with the 'next season'. And in our rush, we dismiss it and discount it. But just as we cannot wish away autumn, winter, spring and summer, we cannot skip over transition. After all, is it not the Lord who changes times and seasons?[24]

A significant portion of David's life teaches us about this underrated season. In 1 Samuel 16:11–13, David, at approximately ten to fifteen years of age, is first anointed king by Samuel the prophet. In 2 Samuel 5:3–5, David finally begins to reign as king; at this point, he's thirty years old. So, what is my point? My point is this: twenty-one chapters represent a fifteen- to twenty-year season of transition in the life of David, yet I read these twenty-one chapters multiple times during the writing of this book. It takes about thirty to forty minutes to read them. It's easy to forget and skim over the fact these chapters are somebody's transition season.

This final part presents four lessons that transition offers us, gleaned from the story of David, which I believe will help you recognise and understand transition when it arrives in your inner world:

1. A lesson on submission and obedience
2. A lesson on authenticity and vulnerability
3. A lesson on conviction and perseverance
4. A lesson on Jesus and His victory

Remember, this sacred season is about being content in the 'now and not yet'.

All will be well. Just learn the lessons.

CHAPTER 17:

Now and Not Yet – Stretch a Little Further

September 2022, Copenhagen, Transition

Flexibility has never been one of my strengths – not including my dexterity from years of violin, piano and recorder playing. Or from typing as an editor and writer. 'Your neck, shoulders, lower back and lower legs are really tense!' I'd received a gift voucher for a full-body massage at Skodsborg Spa Hotel up north from Copenhagen for my fortieth birthday in May 2021. As the masseuse declared the verdict and got to work, my mind drifted to the yoga and Pilates classes I regularly went to during my university days in Melbourne. They'd been my attempt at addressing my lack of flexibility and keeping the tension under control. I stopped practising yoga and Pilates when I moved to Sydney.

I got back into yoga during the COVID-19 pandemic; with everything in a state of lockdown, one of my friends – a yoga instructor – started offering live sessions via Zoom on a Tuesday evening. Those classes met many needs during that time of uncertainty. A family of four in an apartment 24/7, limited interaction with friends and cancelled events. Once a week, for one hour, I got one whole room to myself, conversations with other women, exercise, peace and quiet, and relaxation. Bliss. Well, let's just start with sanity. Unable to clearly assess through a screen what everyone was doing, my instructor gave more verbal instructions than usual and asked more questions about how our bodies were feeling.

'Remember,' she cautioned, 'you can't extend yourself to the point of injury! When you stretch within a pose, keep going until it gets a bit uncomfortable, then pause and inhale, and on the exhale, lean into it just a little bit more and stretch a little further. Then stop there!'

Transition always involves a stretch. Whether you like it or not. Whether you initiate it or not. And as uncomfortable as it is, the way to keep living in transition is to keep living in the stretch. And what was first hard will slowly ease as the tension's released. Flexibility is a moving target, isn't it? Just when you think you're flexible, another pose comes along, proving otherwise. But that's the point. God continues to ask something of us which takes us to yet another level of mastering flexibility – not snapping under pressure.

So, what's God been asking of me during my own season of transition? In the space between the 'now' and 'not yet'?

To get good at awkward, difficult and painful conversations. To get my brave on. To further remove masks designed for people-pleasing and self-preservation. To fear people less and trust God more. To speak assertively, without pendulum swinging between passivity and aggression. To recognise – and eventually, to accept – that we all end up being the villain in another's narrative from time to time. To allow even my opposition to see me cry and to hear unpolished words of anguish come out of my mouth, knowing that vulnerability is what eventually builds bridges of peace and reconciliation.

To pause. To inhale. To exhale. To stretch a little further. To choose to do it all over again until 'not yet' is 'now'.

A lesson on submission and obedience

Shortly after David is anointed the future king, he must first serve and submit to the current king, King Saul. It's ironic, but not coincidental. David is about to observe a king in action. He's about to look up to someone who is already doing what he is going to be doing in the future. This takes place in transition – submitting to an authority he was yet to become and obeying an authority he was yet to have.

King Saul unfortunately becomes greatly jealous of David. In fact, he attempts to kill David several times, and David also receives two opportunities to kill him.[25] Both times he ultimately submits to and obeys the Lord, knowing it is not for him to kill the Lord's anointed king. When transition enters your inner world, be prepared to face difficult decisions – to submit, or not; to obey, or not.

When transition enters your inner world, teaching you about submission and obedience, remember this, dear reader:

God is faithful and will fulfil His promise.

> And David came to Saul and entered his service. And Saul loved him greatly, and he became his armour-bearer. And Saul sent to Jesse, saying, "Let David remain in my service, for he has found favor in my sight."
>
> 1 Samuel 16:21–22 ESV

David may have found Saul's temporary favour, yet He had God's eternal favour. David learned that if it was God who had anointed him, it would be God who would bring it to pass at the right time and in the right way. The same goes for you.

CHAPTER 18:

Now and Not Yet – Show Me Your Friends

December 2022, Copenhagen, Transition

Your relationships and friendships may change when you start being true to who God has created you to be. Some might come to an abrupt end. Some might unexpectedly flourish. Some might gradually shift into another concentric circle – a little further from or a little closer to the core. They'll certainly reveal their insecurities, maturity, faith level, character substance, mindsets and desires as they watch you transform.

American businessman Daniel Peña said, 'Show me your friends, and I'll show you your future.' I once said this phrase to my daughter when she was in the second grade and beginning the hard work of understanding the personalities of her little friends. She looked at me blankly. 'What does that mean, Mummy? Do my friends know my future?' Confusion. A bit of panic flashed on her face. Reassurance immediately needed. 'No, they don't know your future,' I replied. 'It means that the types of friends you have really impact on the type of person you become. And that will impact on your future.' Understanding replaced the panic. 'Friendships must be so much easier when you're grown up, right, Mummy?' I half-smiled, half-grimaced. We continued colouring in, both lost in our own thoughts.

You get to a point where your desperation for change is stronger than your need to be liked and understood. When the consistent voice, gently and firmly beckoning 'Come away with me', is more compelling than the everchanging social media trends screaming 'Follow, like, comment now!' That's called a crossroads. I've been there many times, but the most recent was, of course, at the time of writing these very words. I even drew the concentric circles. Listed names. Drew a picture that apparently reveals my 'future'. I looked at it for a long time, as one does in a gallery – taking small steps backwards, eyes locked on the masterpiece hanging on the wall. Distance and careful consideration. I liked a lot of what I saw – but not everything. I saw interesting patterns. I also noticed gaps that should be filled. I mourned over names that were no longer as close to the core, and reflected on why some were closer than they perhaps ought to be. So, how do you begin to add and move names? Pick up the phone. Send a message. Send an email. Meet for coffee. Say you want more. Or less. Seek to understand their needs, expectations and limitations. Ask brave and curious questions.

If Jesus is at the centre, then that will attract some and repel others. My unique pursuit of Him through my valleys, up my mountains, at my peaks, is changing my picture. And I'm liking what I'm seeing. Liking the names on the 'recent' lists on my iPhone. Looking forward to time with the names on my calendar. So, dear reader, show me your friends. I'll show you who you are comfortable being. Show me the people who have remained with you on your pathway as you pursue the one who beckons 'Come.' That's your future.

A lesson on authenticity and vulnerability

Many of you will be familiar with David's great battle against Goliath, whom he defeats.[26] What's interesting is that he wins through remaining true to himself, not according to the expectations of others. As David is getting ready to face Goliath, King Saul clothes him with armour, even though David has never fought in armour. Can you imagine this young boy wearing a heavy coat of armour? Unsuitably heavy – like many of the expectations and opinions of others that we reluctantly put on.

What does David do? He takes off the armour and sticks with what he knows – a staff, five smooth stones, his pouch and his sling. He approaches the Philistine, and with just one stone and his sling, he knocks Goliath to the ground. His victory required authenticity in the face of other people's ways of doing things. David knew he wasn't going to beat this giant with their strategies; he had to be true to the experiences and skills he already had.

Vulnerability is another trait that develops within David during his transition season. 1 Samuel 18 and 1 Samuel 20 detail David's precious friendship with Jonathan. We see a friendship in which they laugh together and cry together. What's phenomenal is that Jonathan is the son of King Saul. His very own father is the one who wants David dead, and Jonathan is caught between being King Saul's son and David's best friend. Talk about the authenticity, vulnerability and challenging conversations we perhaps don't get to read about in Scripture!

Everything they went through involved genuine fellowship. And that often takes place in the underrated season of transition. You see, when we *do* know what's going on – when we're in autumn or winter or spring or summer – we feel some sense of control and our guards go up. But when transition arrives in our inner world, we're confronted by our need for real community – and that requires authenticity and vulnerability.

When transition enters your inner world, developing authenticity and vulnerability, remember this, dear reader:

People's expectations are not your primary focus.

> Then Saul clothed David with his armor. He put a helmet of bronze on his head and clothed him with a coat of mail, and David strapped his sword over his armor. And he tried in vain to go, for he had not tested them. Then David said to Saul, "I cannot go with these, for I have not tested them." So David put them off. Then he took his staff in his hand and chose five smooth stones from the brook and put them in his shepherd's pouch. His sling was in his hand, and he approached the Philistine.
>
> 1 Samuel 17:38–40 ESV

Transition forced David to face who he truly was. He knew that the only way to move forward was to be comfortable in his own skin, even if that meant not embracing the majority. And through it all, God provided him with a friend in Jonathan, who would see him through. And He will do the same for you.

CHAPTER 19:

Now and Not Yet – Rip Currents

February 2022, Copenhagen, Transition

Most babies in Australia start swimming lessons before they're even old enough to say 'swim' or 'pool'. Water safety is a major thing in the land of Vegemite, Tim Tams and the Sydney Opera House, considering many backyards have pools and Australian beaches are an all-year-round attraction. I still remember mantras from childhood – 'No running around the pool; we walk.'

Things get more serious when it comes to the Aussie oceans. Have you ever heard of a rip current? They're one of the greatest, and most common, hazards on Australian beaches, causing people to drown every year. But what are they, exactly? A rip is a water current that occurs near beaches with breaking waves. It's a strong, narrow and localised current that moves away from the shore. Contrary to how it seems, rip currents don't pull people under the water; they pull people in the opposite direction of the shore. People get dragged under because they begin to panic (understandably) and fight against the current in their attempt to get back to the safety of the beach. That's exhausting, even for a strong swimmer. That's why the best thing you can do is to stay calm, and, if you can, swim parallel to the shore until you're free of the rip. Then you can head for shore and, hopefully, live to tell the tale.

Perpetual rip currents featured prominently in key areas of my life during 2022. Some private, some public. I still feel the ripple effects now. A lot of months spent in the deep unknown, being tossed and turned without a break, struggling for breath only to swallow yet another mouthful of salt water. Countless others get caught in the rips, but that's no help or comfort. Faced collectively, experienced individually. Tragedy, crisis, trauma, calamity, disaster. Whatever word you choose to describe a set of events that turn your life on its head, it will have blindsided you and knocked the wind out of you. I think I've responded to collective and deeply personal rips in a myriad of ways. I've fought the waves. *This isn't gonna take me out; I'm stronger than this.* I've tried ignoring the currents, pretending I'm not drifting away. *Everything's fine, really.* I've swallowed another mouthful of salt water. *It's good for me.* I've tried to drag others in with me. *Why aren't they affected by this? Why are they getting away with this?*

But I'm now learning another way. Allowing the rip current to both engulf me and carry me away. Allowing my body to remain still – to go with the current. To wait for the lifeguard, who will come at just the right moment and gently pull me parallel to the shore and set me on a new course – on this side, and the other side, of eternity. Saved, being saved, will be saved.

A lesson on conviction and perseverance

David had to flee for his life and go into hiding several times throughout his transition season. In 1 Samuel 30, we read a heart-breaking account of David's experience. David and his army return to the city they were based in, only to discover David's enemies have burnt it to the ground, taken their wives and children captive and stolen all their possessions. David's men, who are already exhausted, are overwhelmed by what they have come home to. They want to turn against David; they want to kill him.

What would you do in this situation? Do you want to know what David does? Remarkably, during crisis, Scripture tells us that he 'strengthened himself in the Lord' and 'inquired of the Lord'. When transition enters your inner world, your source of strength, courage and guidance for holding onto your conviction and persevering can only be Him.

When transition enters your inner world, testing conviction and perseverance, remember this, dear reader:
Strength and direction come from God.

> And David was greatly distressed, for the people spoke of stoning him, because all the people were bitter in soul, each for his sons and daughters. But David strengthened himself in the Lord his God...And David inquired of the Lord, "Shall I pursue after this band? Shall I overtake them?" He answered him, "Pursue, for you shall surely overtake and shall surely rescue." So David set out...

1 Samuel 30:6, 8–9a ESV

David strengthens himself in the Lord. David inquires of the Lord. That is his default reaction, which has been developed over time and is now being tested in this transition season. We see his conviction and perseverance. He does not give up; he goes to his source. What does that mean for you? It means not bowing down to what's happening around you and inside of you. It means looking up. It means asking God for strength and for what He would like to say to you in that moment. And He will respond – and lead you back to shore.

CHAPTER 20:

Now and Not Yet – I Can See Clearly Now

July 2022, Innsbruck, Transition

Driving from Copenhagen to Venice looks straightforward on a map. A solid blue line cutting through the green masses representing land. The four of us got into our fully loaded car and drove away from our apartment on a Friday afternoon. We ate dinner on a ferry headed for Germany, then Andrew and I took turns driving through the night while our children slept. Berlin, Leipzig, Nuremberg and Munich were blurs as we drove along the autobahns. In the early hours of Saturday morning, the Austrian Alps came into full view. Andrew pulled over into a McDonald's in Innsbruck for breakfast; the children yawned and rubbed their sleepy eyes.

When you live in a flat city (a cyclist's dream), the sight of mountains right in front of you takes your breath away. With full stomachs, we continued the final six hours through the Alps, getting ready to cross over into Italy's north coast. Now what I am about to write may not seem that significant to you. Underwhelming, even. But it was the first time I'd ever experienced such a sudden, jarring shift in climate and weather. Literally within minutes. One moment, we were driving in temperatures between ten and fifteen degrees, with drizzle falling from grey skies. And then, it happened. Our car emerged from the last mountain tunnel, and I watched in sheer amazement as the dashboard updated the outside temperature every couple of seconds –

seventeen degrees, twenty degrees, twenty-three degrees. Twenty-five. Twenty-eight. Thirty. Thirty-three degrees! Clear blue skies excitedly greeted us as we squinted from the glare of golden sunshine. 'What just happened?' Frederik exclaimed. 'We've shifted from the mountains to the coast,' Andrew explained. 'I can see clearly now! It's so bright!' came the response. Joy in children is a delight.

It can take a long time for something to suddenly change. Tears to laughter, sorrow to joy, longing to fulfilment, despair to celebration. Waiting for an arrival. Old to new. Death to life. Crucifixion to resurrection. We can waste years of our lives by only living for points of origin and destination. What happens in between – the solid blue line – matters the most. Take heart, dear reader; it will all make sense one day. When we stand with unveiled faces, beholding sheer beauty, majesty and light. We will see clearly.

A lesson on Jesus and His victory

Do you want to experience the full benefit of autumn, winter, spring and summer? This is only possible if you choose to value transition. The pause at the very end of an exhale before the next inhale. So much of the wrestle, the discontent, the frustration and the discomfort can be put to rest when we value transition equally to the other four seasons. Autumn, transition, winter, transition, spring, transition, summer, transition, and so the cycle goes on. Seeing the progression of our inner world this way is truly transformational.

There will be many of you reading this who need to know that there are still exciting seasons ahead for you. You need to know that some of your greatest days are still ahead of you. It may not look how you once imagined it, but God, through His providence, is still making a way, weaving the joys, the sorrows, the hopes, the disappointments, the regrets, the fears, the frailties, the successes, the mistakes and the choices into your story of redemption.

When transition enters your inner world, revealing Jesus and His victory, remember this, dear reader:

The old has passed away and the new has come.

> Therefore, if anyone is in Christ, he is a new creation. The old has passed away; behold, the new has come.
>
> 2 Corinthians 5:17 ESV

When you're feeling weary and exhausted, you need to remember that, as followers of Jesus, you've already experienced the greatest transition of all through the death and resurrection of our Lord and Saviour, Jesus Christ. But by the grace of God and the sacrifice of Jesus, you would never be able to make the transition from an eternity separated from God to an eternity in His presence. Indeed, a relationship with Jesus is the greatest transition of all.

PART V –

Cadence

A lesson on submission and obedience: God is faithful and will fulfil His promise.
A lesson on authenticity and vulnerability: People's expectations are not your primary focus.
A lesson on conviction and perseverance: Strength and direction come from God.
A lesson on Jesus and His victory: The old has passed away and the new has come.

CONCLUSION:

Orbit Around the Sun

In the introduction, I asked you what your favourite season is. I wonder what your answer was back then, and what it is now. I also wonder what season you would say you are in right now as you read these final pages. A lot takes place over the course of a year – the 365-day orbit around the sun. Just as our earth experiences its seasons while it circles around the sun, our inner world experiences its seasons with our Triune God – the Father, the Son and the Holy Spirit – at the centre of it all.

Time, invitation, decision, action and lessons. The One who holds your life – and all its seasons – in the safe palms of His hands, is the One who helps us makes sense of time during autumn's loss, extends an invitation to see winter's light, gives us the courage to make decisions in response to spring's hope, strengthens us for action during summer's harvest and opens our spiritual eyes to the lessons of transition's value.

Autumn – understand the pain and preparation of loss.
Winter – learn in the dark how to be light.
Spring – hold onto the promises of hope.
Summer – gather in the harvest.
Transition – be content in the 'now and not yet'.

It's the pilgrimage, which only ends when our time on earth has ceased. Step by step, a little bit closer. Stories lived. Christ being formed within us.

Within every season.

AFTERWORD:

Unforced Rhythms

March 2024, Copenhagen, Spring

The fact you chose to read this book to the end blows me away. I wonder what stories you would share with me from the seasons of your own life if we were sitting opposite each other, perhaps in a bookshop, having an unrushed conversation. Speaking of local bookshops – the owner of Books & Company knows me well. A chai latte; an armchair facing the window; sunshine streaming through, creating shadows on the cream floorboards; surrounded by thousands of books; jazz music playing softly in the background; and my laptop. I turned up one afternoon during spring break to finish writing the book you are now about to finish reading.

Red and green buds cover the branches of the tree in the courtyard, and flowers are starting to blossom in the bookshop's gardens. Spring is here, and I feel that spring has also arrived in my inner world. 2023 was mainly filled with autumn – change, unknowns, preservation and letting go. It felt endless and excruciating. You would have thought I'd have been able to reassure myself that the season would eventually come to an end. But even the author of a book about seasons grows weary and can feel like autumn will be autumn forever. I stopped seeing the importance of the season I found myself in. I forgot that autumn's loss lays the foundation for summer's harvest. When you forget, thank the Lord for community and authentic friendships – for people who come alongside and lovingly remind you of the words you have spoken and written.

And sure enough, at the right time, the birds began to sing again for me. I sensed hope and new possibilities again. You see, we cannot force seasons to come and go. There is a rhythm we cannot control. We must trust the Creator of the seasons – the One who is ultimately weaving together our seasons into our unique story. The One who says, 'Walk with me and work with me—watch how I do it. Learn the unforced rhythms of grace. I won't lay anything heavy or ill-fitting on you. Keep company with me and you'll learn to live freely and lightly.'[27]

If you look with intention, you will see God's fingerprints everywhere – the evidence of what He was doing all along, even when you couldn't see it, hear it and feel it. I don't know what lies ahead, but I know the Lord does, and I trust He is already at work. It's the same for you, too. Keep on going, dear reader. Keep walking with Him. Your story is still being written.

GRATITUDE

Behind every author are people who make the published book possible. My writing journey and this book are no different. I never could have accomplished this on my own. Nor would I have wanted to.

Thank you, Andrew – my 'strength and stay'. I love you more than words can express. Thank you for walking alongside me throughout this entire book project. You witnessed the early mornings as I wrestled with words, handed me cups of coffee, encouraged me to keep going when I wanted to stop (many times), read the early drafts, gave helpful feedback and celebrated the completion of every stage of this process. You are the best husband in the world!

Thank you, Annika – my bright shining star. I am so thankful you are my daughter. Your words of encouragement and excitement about your mum writing a book bless me more than you realise. You are already navigating the seasons of life with strength and courage. I am so proud of you!

Thank you, Frederik – my affectionate son. I will never forget those mornings when you would wake up, walk into the dining room, where I was up early working on this book, climb onto my lap, rest your head against my shoulder and watch me type another sentence. Your cuddles are the best!

Thank you, Clifford and Evelyn Fitt – my dad and mum. You both sacrificed so much to give me the childhood and upbringing that laid a firm foundation for the life I am living now. Thank you for being remarkable examples of resilience, bravery and unwavering faith. I love you both very much!

Thank you, Claire Nogic – a true friend, who has gone the distance and remained steadfast in every season. You've been a witness to many of the stories shared in this book. Your loyalty, generosity, wisdom, encouragement and humour are a gift, and I am so thankful for decades of friendship – and more decades to come!

Thank you to the 'Tribe' – Sharon Anderson, Leslea Petersen, Lisbeth Malmkjær Houlberg, Carriene Rendbo, Anne-Laure Lunsford, Nadia Steyn and Brena Andres. We've gathered around the table for dinner more times than I can count, cried lots of tears, laughed hysterically, prayed for each other, kept WhatsApp in business and supported one another through the highs and lows. Let's keep doing that.

Thank you, Susanne Vind – my psychiatrist who helped me pick up the pieces when it all fell apart. I am grateful for your professional help, guidance and generosity.

Thank you to the members of my two groups of beta readers – Robert Fergusson, Shanelle Hall, Maria Ieroianni, Sandra Hultén, Lasse Ketelsen, Christina Anderson, Rafael Tsai, Greg Andrew, Katie Strong and Marie-Eve Will. Your invaluable feedback, perspectives and ideas helped me shape this book into its final version.

Thank you, Yasmin Yarwood, for your meticulous proof-editing skills; Carlos Darby, for your exceptional creative direction during the book design stage; Hazel Lam, for capturing the essence of my words through beautiful visual imagery; Stuart Smith, for your publication skills; and Sylva Bocsa, for knowing how to make me feel comfortable during a photo shoot!

Thank you, Gabriela Holmgren, for your continual encouragement in the early days to write a book; and Helena Sjölin Lauridsen, for surprising me with a custom-made journal in which all the planning for this book took place. It was the tool I needed to get started.

Thank you, Thomas and Katherine Hansen. I am deeply grateful for the opportunities you gave me to develop and sharpen my spiritual gifts.

Thank you, Eric Andersson and Erika Jarander, for warmly embracing the Mina family; we are excited about what's ahead.

Thank you to the congregations who listened to me preach the *Seasons* sermon series for the first time. We had no idea it was a book in the making!

Finally, thank you to my Triune God – the Father, the Son and the Holy Spirit. The ultimate author, you gave me these words, and I now trust you to make them known so that you alone are glorified.

SEASONS SUMMARY

AUTUMN'S LOSS

A time of transition and change: God remains the same.
A time of mystery and unknowns: God is still at work.
A time of preservation and protection: God knows what you need next.
A time of letting go and receiving comfort: God is your comforter.

WINTER'S LIGHT

An invitation to draw closer: establish spiritual disciplines.
An invitation to go deeper: deepen relationships.
An invitation to grow stronger: persevere through challenge and wait patiently for change.
An invitation to shine brighter: bring hope to others.

SPRING'S HOPE

A decision to take steps of faith: bravely act on your dreams.
A decision to make plans to bless: intentionally make a difference.
A decision to allow space to simplify: honestly examine your inner world.
A decision to look ahead with expectation: confidently place your hope in Jesus.

SUMMER'S HARVEST

An action to bring in your abundance: involves faithfulness, strategy and hard work.
An action to stand firm in your field: involves obstacles, challenge and adversity.
An action to kneel on your threshing floor: involves separation, sacrifice and surrender.
An action to lift your eyes to new horizons: involves fresh vision, opportunity and change.

TRANSITION'S VALUE

A lesson on submission and obedience: God is faithful and will fulfil His promise.
A lesson on authenticity and vulnerability: People's expectations are not your primary focus.
A lesson on conviction and perseverance: Strength and direction come from God.
A lesson on Jesus and His victory: The old has passed away and the new has come.

REFLECT ON YOUR SEASON –

Journaling Prompts and Practical Tips

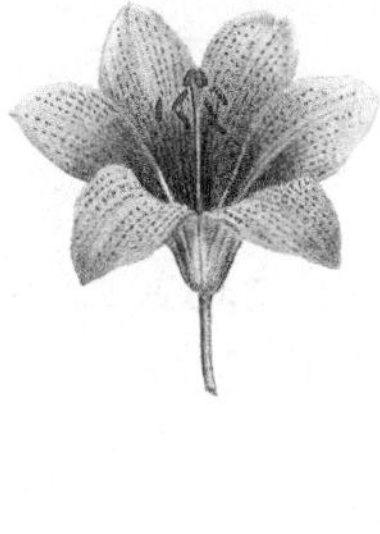

PART I – AUTUMN'S LOSS

1. A time of transition and change: God remains the same.

Journaling Prompt

How do you typically respond to endings and beginnings?

What great loss shapes and influences you to this very day, and in what ways?

Practical Tip

Start a gratitude journal. Every morning or every evening, whether in a notebook or on your phone, write down two things from the past twenty-four hours you are grateful for. Over time, this will turn into a record of the miraculous ways in which God has turned up in your life. Your gratitude journal will become something you go back to and read over – your reminder of your God who changes not.

2. A time of mystery and unknowns: God is still at work.

Journaling Prompt

We often don't see what God was up to all along until the right amount of time has passed. Then the light-bulb moment takes place, and we see the final puzzle piece placed in its correct spot. Can you remember a time when this happened to you? If not, how would your current perspective change if you embraced the mystery?

Practical Tip

Do a Bible word study on the term 'providence', then read through the narrative recounts of Joseph (Genesis 37–50), Ruth (Ruth 1–4) and Esther (Esther 1–10).

3. A time of preservation and protection: God knows what you need next.

Journaling Prompt

How comfortable are you about acknowledging your needs and taking care of your soul?

How does this perspective on autumn being a time of preservation and protection affect your attitude towards winter?

Practical Tip

In addition to your daily Bible reading and prayer, do something to aid your spiritual growth:

- Think about an area you want to grow in or a topic you want to learn more about.
- Find some resources and dig in – there's no shortage of books, podcasts, websites, Bible studies, online courses, webinars and events to choose from!

4. A time of letting go and receiving comfort: God is your comforter.

Journaling Prompt

How do you handle facing your limitations, weaknesses and imperfections, and how do you process your failures and regrets?

Practical Tip

Take time to be by yourself and read 2 Corinthians 1:3–7 from two or three different Bible versions. And read them out loud; let your ears hear your voice declaring the words. Ask God to comfort you and to help you let go of things that are no longer yours to carry.

PART II – WINTER'S LIGHT

1. An invitation to draw closer: establish spiritual disciplines.

Journaling Prompt

God is your source of hope, strength, wisdom and power. What situations cause you to withdraw from Him and others?

Practical Tip

- **Kick-start daily Bible reading:** Read through the book of Proverbs in one month. Proverbs has 31 chapters filled with wisdom, insight and principles for everyday living. Don't wait for the first day of the month. If today is the seventh of the month, just go to Chapter 7!

- **Worship:** Find your soundtrack or create a season playlist and let it minister your soul and lead you in worship.

- **Pray with others:** During your challenging season, bravely reach out to people to pray with. You don't have to tell them all the details. And I don't mean ask them to pray for you on their own (though that's important, too), but to actually meet up with you in person, online or over the phone so you can pray together.

2. An invitation to go deeper: deepen relationships.

Journaling Prompt

Is it easy or difficult for you to open up and allow others to get to know the real you? Why?

What 'masks' or 'armour' do you put on, and what purpose do they serve?

Practical Tip

We all need a community of believers whom we share life with. This usually starts around the table, sharing a meal, asking curious questions, genuinely listening to answers and willingly opening up. Who knows – perhaps, out of your current winter, some of your most precious relationships will emerge! Organise a social engagement for the week ahead – one-on-one or in a group.

3. An invitation to grow stronger: persevere through challenge and wait patiently for change.

Journaling Prompt

As a child, what did you learn to do for protection which no longer serves you well as an adult?

Practical Tip

Is there a specialist you need to reach out to in this season? Bravely make that first or next appointment, whether it's with a doctor, therapist, personal trainer, financial adviser, spiritual director, nutritionist, business coach or someone else.

4. An invitation to shine brighter: bring hope to others.

Journaling Prompt

Can you remember a story someone once told you which encouraged you? What was it? How did it give you hope?

Practical Tip

Tell someone your story of God at work in your life.

PART III – SPRING'S HOPE

1. A decision to take steps of faith: bravely act on your dreams.

Journaling Prompt

Who do you want to become? What do you want your life to look like? How do you want to use your skills, time and resources? What changes do you want to make in the different areas of your life?

Practical Tip

Pray and ask God to give you brilliant ideas. Take time to write down your dreams. Then, write down the next step you need to make to start acting on those dreams and ideas.

2. A decision to make plans to bless: intentionally make a difference.

Journaling Prompt

What great need do you see in your community, in your nation and/or in the world that you would love to meet if there were no limitations on your time, talent and treasure?

Practical Tip

Consider the time, skills, finances and possessions you have in this season. Think of one thing you can do that would be an intentional blessing. Plan it, schedule it and do it!

3. A decision to allow space to simplify: honestly examine your inner world.

Journaling Prompt

How would you describe the health of each of these five areas in your life?

1. Thoughts and mindset
2. Emotions
3. Attitudes
4. Habits and daily disciplines
5. Relationships

Practical Tip

Reach out to someone who can be your accountability partner on your journey of examining the state of your inner world – someone who can listen without judgement, ask curious questions and pray for you.

4. A decision to look ahead with expectation: confidently place your hope in Jesus.

Journaling Prompt

What situation, relationship or decision do you need to place in the hands of Jesus?

Practical Tip

Whether it's in a notebook or on a device, put aside some time to revise your current goals or set new ones. Spring is the perfect time to do so!

PART IV – SUMMER'S HARVEST

1. An action to bring in your abundance: involves faithfulness, strategy and hard work.

Journaling Prompt

What holds you back from making the most of an opportunity?

What is your attitude towards hard work?

Practical Tip

Whether it's your work, studies, family, relationships, finances or another area, create a strategy that will enable you to actively pursue and be faithful with what God has placed in your life.

2. An action to stand firm in your field: involves obstacles, challenge and adversity.

Journaling Prompt

What does the phrase 'stand firm' mean to you right now?

Practical Tip

The Bible teaches us that it's not always flesh and blood. We need to learn how to fight spiritual battles spiritually, not naturally. Study Ephesians 6 – read the chapter slowly and several times through. Write down your observations and how the chapter applies to your season. Look up commentaries that analyse and unpack this portion of Scripture.

3. An action to kneel on your threshing floor: involves separation, sacrifice and surrender.

Journaling Prompt

What price have you paid in the past to move forward into your future? How did that turn out?

What thoughts and feelings do the words 'sacrifice', 'separation' and 'surrender' bring up?

Practical Tip

Delayed obedience is still disobedience. If the Holy Spirit has asked you to do something, but you're putting it off, now's the time to do it!

4. An action to lift your eyes to new horizons: involves fresh vision, opportunity and change.

Journaling Prompt

What recent accomplishments and successes have you achieved?

How do your body and mind respond once a productive season has concluded?

Practical Tip

Pay fresh attention to what is going on around and within you during this time – circumstances, conversations, 'coincidences', unexpected changes, new longings and desires.

PART V – TRANSITION'S VALUE

1. A lesson on submission and obedience: God is faithful and will fulfil His promise.

Journaling Prompt

Do submission and obedience come naturally to you? Why or why not?

Are there any promises that you realise may not be for this side of eternity?

Practical Tip

Consider the people and positions you currently submit to and obey – personally, professionally and in general society. Now, consider your attitude towards those people and positions. Remember it is ultimately God who you are submitting to and obeying.

2. A lesson on authenticity and vulnerability: people's expectations are not your primary focus.

Journaling Prompt

What do you think and feel about the circles and names you've drawn?

In what areas of your life are you needing to be true to who God has created you to be?

What friendships are you intentionally building now that you'll need in the future?

Practical Tip

Draw three concentric circles in your journal to take stock of the people currently in your world.

The smallest circle in the middle is for the names of those closest to you – your spouse, family members and best friends. The ones whom you are sharing the journey of life with, often share meals around the table with.

The medium circle is for the names of people who may still be a regular part of your life, but without the same degree of closeness as the inner circle – people you chat with every Sunday at church, your work colleagues, peers you study with, those you share a sport or hobby with.

The largest circle is for the names of those we hold at a distance for unfortunate reasons (the estranged family relative) or people you'd like to move into the medium circle (parents of kids in your child's class) or acquaintances you see from time to time (your hairdresser).

3. A lesson on conviction and perseverance: strength and direction come from God.

Journaling Prompt

What convictions of yours have recently been tested?

What might happen if you chose to persevere rather than give up?

Practical Tip

You need a word from God about your circumstances. We need the Word of the Lord to strengthen us, and we do that by inquiring. It's time to pick up your Bible, ask God to speak to you specifically about your season, and start reading. Don't stop until you get that word which is going to sustain you.

4. A lesson on Jesus and His victory: the old has passed away and the new has come.

Journaling Prompt

What transitions are you currently facing?

Are you lacking clarity about anything?

Practical Tip

As a follower of Jesus, you are a new creation! Pray this prayer:

Thank you, Lord, that in Christ, I am a new creation.
The old has passed away, and the new has come.
Please give me clarity, wisdom and perseverance in seasons of transition.
Help me to recognise the lessons to learn, which will enable me to mature in Christ.
Thank you that I can walk in victory.
Amen.

NOTES

[1] Henri Nouwen with Michael J. Chistensen and Rebecca J. Laird. *Spiritual Direction: Wisdom for the Long Walk of Faith* (Great Britain: Society for Promoting Christian Knowledge (SPCK): 2011), 46.
[2] Rabindranath Tagore (born 7 May 1861, Calcutta [now Kolkata], India – died 7 August 1941, Calcutta) was a Bengali poet, short-story writer, song composer, playwright, essayist and painter.
[3] See Genesis 3.
[4] See Ecclesiastes 3:11.
[5] Sonnet accompanying Vivaldi's Concerto no. 3 in F major, RV 293, "AUTUMN" *Allegro (Peasant Dance and Song)/Adagio Molto (Sleeping Drunkards)/Allegro (The Hunt)* published 1725, Amsterdam – English translation of Italian original.
[6] Bessel van der Kolk. *The Body Keeps the Score: Brain, Mind, and Body in the Healing of Trauma* (USA: Penguin Group: 2014).
[7] Elizabeth Levy. *The Gymnasts: #3 Nobody's Perfect* (USA: Scholastic: 1988).
[8] Sonnet accompanying Vivaldi's Concerto no. 4 in F minor, RV 297, "WINTER" *Allegro non molto/Largo/Allegro* published 1725, Amsterdam – English translation of Italian original.
[9] Wayne Cordeiro. *Leading on Empty: Refilling Your Tank and Renewing Your Passion* (USA: Bethany House Publishers: 2009), 70.
[10] Rick Warren. *The Purpose Driven Life*. (USA: Zondervan: 2002).
[11] See John 5:6.
[12] Paul Webster and Sammy Fain. *Calamity Jane: Vocal Score* (Great Britain: Faber Music Ltd: 1989).
[13] *Der findes ikke dårligt vejr, kun dårlig påklædning!*
[14] Sonnet accompanying Vivaldi's Concerto no. 1 in E major, RV 269, "SPRING" *Allegro/Largo/Allegro (Pastorale dance)* published 1725, Amsterdam – English translation of Italian original.

[15] There is a longstanding rivalry between 'Sydneysiders' and 'Melbournians'. For some, it's lighthearted jest; for others, it's serious. This rivalry especially comes out in sport competitions and in debates about which city is better.

[16] Matthew 5:3 MSG.

[17] Ibid.

[18] Sonnet accompanying Vivaldi's Concerto No. 2 in G minor, RV 315, "SUMMER" *Allegro non molto – Allegro/Adagio – Presto – Adagio/Presto (Summer Storm)* published 1725, Amsterdam – English translation of Italian original.

[19] See Galatians 5:22–23.

[20] See Acts 3:19.

[21] See Job 1:21.

[22] See Exodus 3:8.

[23] See Genesis 37–50.

[24] See Daniel 2:21.

[25] See 1 Samuel 24 and 26.

[26] See 1 Samuel 17.

[27] See Matthew 11:28–30 MSG.

Celina Evelyn Mina is a preacher, teacher and writer, and loves helping people apply biblical principles to everyday living. She is a part of the communication team at her local church, ARK CPH. Celina is a gifted communicator known for the way she unpacks Scripture and weaves personal stories into her messages to illustrate the relevance and power of the Bible in all areas of life. Based in Copenhagen, Denmark (but always an Aussie at heart!), Celina is married with two children and enjoys reading, going to concerts and exhibitions, being by the ocean, having meaningful conversations and drinking chai lattes. *Seasons: Stories of Loss, Light, Hope and Harvest* is her first book.

Website: celinamina.com
Instagram: @celinamina
LinkedIn: /celinamina

Printed in Great Britain
by Amazon

55600980R00106